The WRIGHT WAY

The WRIGHT WAY

7 Problem-Solving Principles
from the Wright Brothers That
Can Make Your Business Soar!

MARK EPPLER

AMACOM AMERICAN MANAGEMENT ASSOCIATION
NEW YORK • ATLANTA • BRUSSELS • CHICAGO • MEXICO CITY
SAN FRANCISCO • SHANGHAI • TOKYO • TORONTO • WASHINGTON, D.C.

Special discounts on bulk quantities of AMACOM books are available to corporations, professional associations, and other organizations. For details, contact Special Sales Department, AMACOM, a division of American Management Association, 1601 Broadway, New York, NY 10019.
Tel.: 212-903-8316. Fax: 212-903-8083.
Web site: www.amacombooks.org

This publication is designed to provide accurate and authoritative information in regard to the subject matter covered. It is sold with the understanding that the publisher is not engaged in rendering legal, accounting, or other professional service. If legal advice or other expert assistance is required, the services of a competent professional person should be sought.

LEGO® is a trademark of the LEGO Group; Tinkertoys® is a trademark of Hasbro; and Erector Set® is a trademark of Meccano S.N.

Library of Congress Cataloging-in-Publication Data

Eppler, Mark, 1946–
   The Wright way : seven problem solving principles from the Wright brothers that can make your business soar! / Mark Eppler.
      p. cm.
Includes bibliographical references and index.
ISBN 0-8144-0797-8
   1. Wright, Orville, 1871–1948—Philosophy.   2. Wright, Wilbur, 1867–1912—Philosophy.   3. Aeronautics—Research—United States—History. 4. Problem solving. 5. Success in business. 6. Aeronautical engineers—United States—Biography. I. Title.

TL540.W7E64 2004
658.4'03—dc21

                                                          2003011346

Printing number
10 9 8 7 6 5 4 3 2 1

CONTENTS

PREFACE

ON DECEMBER 17, 2003, aviation experts and enthusiasts of early flight will converge on a small hamlet on the Outer Banks of North Carolina to pay homage to two of America's most famous citizens, Wilbur and Orville Wright. The cause of their journey will be the centennial celebration of what many believe to be the event of the century: history's first heavier-than-air, powered and controlled flight. The celebration will culminate at 10:35 A.M. at the Wright Brothers National Memorial, four miles south of Kitty Hawk at Kill Devil Hills. If all goes according to plan, an authentic reproduction of the original *Wright Flyer* will glide along a sixty-foot monorail and rise into the Carolina sky, just as Orville Wright did a hundred years earlier.

As American heroes go, the status of the Wright brothers is iconic. Long before the media began hyping the first flight centennial, Wilbur and Orville Wright had what marketing experts call "brand" recognition. At one time, the brothers were the two most famous men in the world. Today, they rank with Presidents Lincoln and Washington in terms of public awareness. Ask any elementary school student who the inventor of the airplane was and he'll most likely reply, "The Wright brothers." Yet our comprehension of their achievement remains shallow, the significance of the event obscured by the celebrity of the brothers themselves.

Hopefully, the centennial celebration will remedy that, because what Wilbur and Orville Wright accomplished should be known, understood, and, most important, *learned from*.

In terms of its capacity to inspire, few achievements can match what these modest bicycle builders from Dayton, Ohio, accomplished. Orville's twelve-second journey, which took place in near obscurity, would become man's most visible evidence to date that the impossible could indeed be accomplished. The first flight not only redefined our world, it redefined the human spirit. These were, as Charles Lindbergh described them, the "log cabin days of aviation," the dawning of a new generation of pioneers who would chase horizons from the sandy beaches of the Outer Banks to the powdery lunar terrain of Tranquility Base.

Read All About It

To say much has been written about the Wright brothers is an understatement. Log onto your local library's website, tag the NavBar for Research Databases, and hop on over to the Books-in-Print site. Type in the keywords "Wright+Brothers," and you'll see 302 books currently in print that match the search criteria. When you factor in books out-of-print, articles, cassettes, videotapes, and DVDs, you need a book just to keep track of everything already written about the Wright brothers. In fact, such a book already exists. It's called *Wilbur and Orville Wright: A Bibliography,* by Arthur Renstrom. Published in 1968 by the Library of Congress, thousands of references to Wilbur and Orville are jam-packed on double-column pages.

If you're into biographies and want to learn more about the Wright brothers and their remarkable family history, there are no fewer than eight full treatments available. I recommend *The Bishop's Boys: A Life of Wilbur and Orville Wright,* by Tom Crouch. Crouch's book was the first biography I read after visiting Kitty Hawk and remains, many biographies later, a personal favorite. This takes nothing away from Harry Combs (*Kill Devil Hill: Discovering the Secret of the Wright Brothers*), Fred Howard (*Wilbur and Orville: A Biography of the Wright Brothers*), or Fred Kelly (*The Wright Brothers*), all of which I have enjoyed.

Fred Kelly's book, the only biography authorized by Orville Wright, is an interesting story in itself. Orville had been approached for decades by authors wanting to tell the Wright brothers' story. He had intended to write it himself, fearing no one else would be as meticulous as necessary. Unlike Wilbur, whose enjoyment of writing made him the official Wright brother "scribe," Orville dreaded it, despite the fact that he wrote well. So he put it off. Even strong urging from Charles Lindbergh failed to get things going. Finally, in 1940 Kelly, a friend of twenty-five years and author of twelve books, convinced Orville to let him write the story. Orville agreed, but with the proviso that it be a technical book (he thought no one would be interested in personal stories) and that he would have final say on every detail.

"Writing a book with Orville Wright looking over your shoulder," recalls Ivonette Wright Miller in *Wright Reminiscences,* "would not be an easy task." She knew her uncle well. After several months of working on the book, Orville wearied of the chore and abruptly decided to cancel the project. He offered to pay Kelly for his time if he would agree to call it quits. Kelly forestalled Orville's efforts to back out of the project by asking him a simple question. "Would you," he asked Orville, "have been willing to give up on December 17, 1903?" Orville, whose perseverance and determination had been keys to the first flight, had no alternative but to return to the writing table.

A Local Perspective

Last year, while conducting research in Kitty Hawk, I came across a nice little book that has become one of my favorites. Written in 1993 by Thomas Parramore, professor emeritus at Meredith College, *Triumph at Kitty Hawk* tells the story of the first flight from the perspective of the people present when it happened. Drawing heavily on local sources, Parramore captures the uniqueness (who else calls lying in a prone position "belly bumpums"?) of the Outer Bankers and their relationship with Wilbur and Orville. Parramore makes a compelling case that without the help provided by locals, the advent of the airplane might have been postponed for years. He calls it "benign destiny" that brought the Wright brothers to Kitty Hawk, stating confidently (if not convincingly) that without their support, the discovery of the airplane "might well have gone to some other nation."

All of the Wright brother biographies mentioned touch lightly on the technical aspects of powered, heavier-than-air flight. However, if you're an aviation buff or someone who wants to understand the technical aspects of the brothers' work, the best book to read is Peter Jakab's *Visions of a Flying Machine.* Jakab artfully walks the reader through the details of the invention step-by-step, providing enough formulas and equations to please the most ardent enthusiast. If you want to know how the Wright brothers calculated lift and drag, or how they determined the angle of incidence, Jakab gets the job done. Just about every aspect of the Wright brothers' work has been covered to date, except one: how this extraordinary achievement can be put to use in business today. That is the purpose of this book, and I'd like to tell you how it came about.

First Interest in First Flight

In 1983, I had the privilege of visiting the Wright Brothers National Memorial in Kill Devil Hills, North Carolina. We had planned a brief stop at the memorial, but ended up staying the day, remaining until the steady stream of visitors had gathered souvenirs and left. Lingering on the field, I walked toward two sheds, authentic replicas of the Wright brothers' camp and the world's first airplane hangar. Nearby was a large scalloped stone that marked the exact spot where the historic flights had begun. It was here that the brothers had laid down a starting track that would keep their *Flyer* from getting bogged down in the sand. Although eighty years had passed since that cold December day in 1903 when Orville had "slipped the surly bonds of earth" and flown, the excitement of his twelve-second journey remained, an honored moment captured for all time. That unplanned visit to the site of the first flight was the beginning of a personal "affliction" with the Wright brothers that has lasted two decades.

After I returned from that trip, I began an extensive reading program on the Wright brothers and the history of early flight. Soon, my objective was to see and experience "all things Wright." Such a goal had to begin with a pilgrimage to Washington, D.C., to see the original 1903 *Wright Flyer.* I remember seeing the Wright brothers' flying machine for the first time, hanging from the ceiling of the Smithsonian National Air and Space Museum. As a symbol of America's ingenuity, it has no peer.

Suspended in the main atrium, the *Flyer* "soars" as majestically as the eagles that inspired it.

From the Smithsonian, my journey took me on to Dearborn, Michigan, site of the Henry Ford Museum and Greenfield Village. Concerned that America might lose track of its "seeds of inventive greatness," Ford decided to create a village preserving the homes and business places of its greatest inventors. In 1938, he purchased the original Wright home and bicycle shop and relocated them to his "living" museum. I toured the original Wright home and bicycle shop, then headed south. On a farm near Millville, Indiana, I saw the farm and homestead (restored) where Wilbur was born. I was pleasantly surprised by the museum there, which featured an authentic reproduction of the *Wright Flyer,* as well as an interesting collection of Wright family memorabilia. From there, I followed the family's move to Richmond, Indiana, where Bishop Wright edited a newspaper and son Wilbur attended high school. Then it was time to go to Dayton, the birthplace of flight itself. It was the first of many visits.

Birthplace of Aviation

While Dayton, Ohio, may not be able to claim the first flight, it can lay legitimate claim to its origin. Highlighting its role as the birthplace of aviation, Dayton has created the Aviation Trail, a self-guided tour of the city's considerable aviation history. I began the tour at Huffman Prairie, the former cow pasture near Wright-Patterson Air Force Base, where the Wright brothers perfected their flyers in 1905. I stopped at the Wright Cycle Company at 22 Williams Street on the west side of Dayton, the last original Wright brothers' structure remaining in the city. The drafting table and workbenches used by the brothers give the museum a special feel. From there, it was just a ten-minute drive to Carillon Historical Park, a working village built to honor the Miami Valley's rich farming and industrial history. Among the complex of twenty buildings, visitors find thousands of antiques and artifacts representing the history of the area, including automobiles, trains, canal boats, and bicycles. And an airplane.

The highlight of the park, especially this centennial year, is the section of the village dedicated to the Wright brothers. A replica of the bicycle shop where the Wrights worked and built their first gliders is complete with antique tools and wooden bicycle rims. After touring the shop, the visitor is led down a hallway filled with authentic Wright memorabilia: the camera used to take the famous first flight photo, the sewing machine used to stitch the fabric that covered the craft's wings, the bicycle converted into a test device to measure lift and drag. At the end of the hall, a door leads to an auditorium where the second most important flying machine in history is dramatically displayed. *The Wright Flyer III* is the world's first fully practical airplane. Orville not only offered design ideas for the auditorium, he personally directed restoration of the flying machine itself.

Later, I was fortunate to squeeze in a tour of Orville's Hawthorn Hill mansion in Oakwood, Ohio, where his creative talents are further revealed in his many "home improvement" projects. I paid my respects at the family gravesite at Woodland Cemetery, marveling that the headstones of such towering giants of invention would be so small. The brothers would have it no other way. As I left the cemetery, I noticed a stone bench on the right where two derby hats, the kind the Wright brothers wore, appeared to have been left behind. Cast in bronze and painted black, they were a touching remembrance of the two gentlemen from Dayton who changed the world.

The Wright Brothers' Problem-Solving Model

It wasn't long after my interest in the Wright brothers was first piqued that I began to incorporate their story into my management seminars and workshops. Problem solving is a key component of the management process, and I found many tips that I could share from the life and work of Wilbur and Orville Wright. It wasn't until two years ago, however, that I discovered these tips had coalesced into seven problem-solving principles that seemed to weave their way through each step of the Wright brothers' work. Those principles became the backbone of a stand-alone program I developed on creative problem solving and team building.

Although the Wright brothers have been recognized for inventing the world's first heavier-than-air flying machine, one of their more significant contributions—a viable problem-solving model—has been largely overlooked. Although much has been written about the Wright brothers' invention, nothing has been written that addresses the problem-solving principles they followed in creating it. Principles that, if applied to today's business challenges, could yield the same successful results. The purpose of *The Wright Way* is to rectify that shortcoming.

I hope readers will find *The Wright Way* a motivating book. But if all readers get out of the story is motivation, they will miss an incredible problem-solving guide. On the other hand, if all readers get out of this story is a problem-solving guide, they'll miss out on the force-multiplying capacity of an incredibly inspiring story! My objective in writing this book is to *preserve both*. My goal is not only to share with the reader the problem-solving principles that guided the Wright brothers, but to illustrate and energize each with a portion of their experience and personalities as gleaned from diaries, letters, and the recorded history of their work. In so doing, I would like to add my bit in making the case for the first flight as *the event* of the twentieth century.

Avoiding Circles of Confusion

In writing a book of this nature, it is often helpful to provide a few caveats and comments to clarify what photographic experts call "circles of confusion." To properly illustrate certain points in the book, it was necessary to reference other aviation pioneers. In an effort to provide the reader a frame of reference on these people, I've included a brief bio on each person at the end of the book. Since this book is not a biography, and since certain parts of the Wright brothers' story appear in different chapters, a chronology of events is also included to help the reader understand the sequence in which things actually occurred.

Benjamin Franklin once commented that his ideas were the "collective gleanings" of others. Although no one, to the best of my knowledge, has made a direct connection between the Wright brothers and the need of business to solve problems, many have written excellent books on the Wright brothers themselves. These I have "gleaned" liberally, noting attribution when used. I am providing readers with a bibliography and recommended reading list should they wish to learn more about these extraordinary men.

Caveats

- The reader will notice I have avoided the word *airplane*. In conducting my research, I discovered that the phrase "flying machine" was applied to aerial devices of any kind prior to the development of the 1903 *Wright Flyer.* Although originally used to describe a flat wing surface, the term *aeroplane* came into popular use during the decade following the first flight of Orville Wright. After World War I, aeroplane was eventually replaced with the term we use today. My intent in using the phrase "flying machine" is to make my references the same as what Wilbur and Orville would have used leading up to their historic breakthrough at Kill Devil Hills.
- It's confusing, to those casually familiar with the Wright brothers' story, to hear the site of their triumph identified as Kill Devil Hills. From our earliest school days, we were taught about the Wright brothers at Kitty Hawk. On their first visit to the Outer Banks in 1900, the brothers did set up camp near this small fishing village on the edge of Albemarle Sound. In subsequent years, however, they moved their base of operations four miles south to be closer to the three large dunes—Big Hill, West Hill, and Little Hill—needed to test their gliders. The dunes, and surrounding area, are known collectively as Kill Devil Hills. All references to the site of the first flight are correctly attributed to this area.
- Since the purpose of this book is to highlight what I believe to be the event of the century (the first flight), it does not cover the lives of the Wright brothers beyond December 17, 1903. The reader is encouraged to go on, however, and see how the Wright brothers' problem-solving skills were put to further test as they struggled to protect their patents and build a flying business.
- Since I am not a pilot or authority on the mechanics of flying (my fifteen seconds of fame as a "Wright B" pilot notwithstanding), I have tried to steer clear of using too many aviation terms. Since that's all but impossible in a book of this nature, I have provided a brief glossary of the aviation terms at the back of the book that can be referenced by the novice and ignored by the professional.

➤ Quotes attributed to Wilbur and Orville Wright come from two sources: *The Papers of Wilbur and Orville Wright,* edited by Marvin McFarland, or *The Published Writings of Wilbur and Orville Wright,* edited by Peter Jakab and Rick Young. When a source other than these is used, it is referenced in the text.

➤ Whenever I refer to a company or organization, I do not give its name. My reason is twofold. First, I want to keep the focus on the Wright brothers and how they achieved what they did. Second, things change. Not long after Tom Peters wrote *In Search of Excellence,* many of the companies referenced as "doing it right" had fallen on hard times. It wasn't that long ago that people were singing the praises of Enron. I prefer to let the principles stand on their own merit.

➤ Last, one challenge in writing this book was the number of contradictions in the research material. "The story," Wright biographer Fred Howard notes, "has become encrusted with a fringe of half-truths and outright untruths." Not to mention more than a few errors. For example, one important source says the flying machine used on the first flight was called the *Kitty Hawk Flyer.* Everyone else calls it the *Wright Flyer.* One source calls Otto Lilienthal, an important figure in aviation history, a mechanical engineer. Another says he was a civil engineer. It's minor, but it matters. Knowing that Orville was obsessive about accuracy, I've chased down as many of these discrepancies as possible. If you, the reader, find any others, please let me know about them.

Acknowledgments

A Tribute . . .

This book is dedicated to the memory of Donald Bush, who lost a courageous battle last year to pancreatic cancer. In many respects, Don reminded me of Wilbur Wright. Like Wilbur, he had an insatiable curiosity about the things around him. He functioned effortlessly in the realm of theory, but was happiest when he could get his hands on something. He was a born tinkerer who loved to repair and improve things. An engineer by training, Don became one of the top EMI (electromagnetic interference) scientists in the world. He was a frequent speaker at symposiums throughout North America, Europe, and the Pacific Rim. He was also my brother-in-law. Two days before he slipped into a coma from which he would not recover, he asked me how my book was coming along. I told him it was "simmering." The last words he ever spoke to me were, "Be sure and get it done." I have carried out his request.

. . . And Thanks

Benjamin Franklin once wrote that his work was the "collective gleanings" of other people. There are many people that I've "gleaned" from in putting this book together. I would like to express my appreciation to Dawne Dewey, head of Special Collections at Wright State University, for her gracious assistance. Special thanks to Adrienne Hickey, executive editor of AMACOM Books, for her professional direction and enthusiasm in making it all come together. Most important, I would like to thank my family for their support and encouragement: Carrie and Chad for brainstorming; Stephanie and Rick for accountability; my wife, Linda, for her ideas, encouragement, and patience in listening to all those Wright brothers stories; and my parents, whose main passion for books and ideas made "forever learning" a part of our family culture.

Heavier-than-air flying machines are impossible.
Lord Kelvin, President, The Royal Society of London
June 1885

A man-carrying airplane will eventually be built,
but only if mathematicians and engineers work
steadily for the next one to ten million years.
New York Times editorial
December 1903

Man will fly, but the craft will be the size of a
matchbook and carry an insect for a passenger.
Simon Newcomb, respected scientific authority
December 1903

*   *   *

It is my belief that flight is possible.
Wilbur Wright, bicycle builder
May 1900

INTRODUCTION

INTREPID SOULS

WHILE CONDUCTING research for this book, I came across a picture of an aviation pioneer, a barrel-chested man with a thick beard, standing on the top of a small shed at the summit of a hill. This intrepid soul, embedded in a framework of wood, cotton, and wire that loosely resembled the wings of a bird, was preparing to hurl himself into the sky in an attempt to fly. As I looked at the man and his flying apparatus, I was reminded of the news shorts that used to precede the featured attraction at the movies. The ones that showed those crazy men and their flying machines in fast speed, making them look like comic characters from the Keystone Kops. We laughed at the lunacy of their efforts, amazed that these people would risk their lives in such fashion. It never occurred to us that these weren't escapees from the nearest asylum, but some of the best and brightest—

not to mention courageous—scientists and engineers trying to solve the greatest problem of the age: heavier-than-air manned flight.

Sacrifices Were Made

The man standing on the top of the shed in the picture I was looking at was Otto Lilienthal, the owner of a small manufacturing company on the outskirts of Berlin. Lilienthal's considerable abilities as an engineer and mathematician enabled him to make an invaluable contribution to the science of flight. Carefully logging the information gleaned from each attempt, Lilienthal completed more than 2,000 glides before suffering a fatal crash on August 6, 1896. His calculations on the lift and drag of various airfoils (wings) would guide future experimenters in their efforts to conquer the skies. Moments before he died from the injuries suffered in his accident, Lilienthal reportedly uttered the words later etched on his tombstone: *"Opfer mussen gebracht werden."* Sacrifices must be made.

Lilienthal, whose exploits had been captured by a print media just beginning to use actual photographs instead of etchings in its coverage, was the first man in history to make soaring glides of any distance. Dramatic pictures of the "flying man" had appeared in newspapers and magazines worldwide, causing his passing to be widely noted and mourned. In Dayton, Ohio, Wilbur and Orville Wright, who had followed Lilienthal's experiments with growing interest, were saddened by his sudden death. At the same time, however, they were inspired by his courage and passionate belief in the possibility of manned flight. Wilbur, who later would claim to be "afflicted" by that same belief, would attribute his first active interest in soaring flight (gliding) to the experiments of Otto Lilienthal.

Curiosity Piqued

When Wilbur's interest in flight was first aroused, he did what he and his brother had always done when something intrigued them: He searched for information on the subject. He began by reading material available in the family library, including a book by Etienne Jules Marey called *Animal Mechanism*. Disappointed by its lack of detail on the mechanics of flight, he nevertheless read it several times looking for connections. Scientific articles in the two encyclopedias, *Chambers and Britannica,* kept in their living room were of little help, either. Even the Dayton library had been a disappointment, its collection displaying little interest in the subject. The need to attend to a growing business, however, reduced Wilbur's research to an occasional article or discussion with Orville. "The spark of curiosity flickered over the next two years," Tom Crouch writes in *The Bishop's Boys,* "but it did not die."

Wilbur's interest in manned flight was rekindled in 1899 after reading some books on ornithology. Hoping to increase his understanding, Wilbur, binoculars in hand, began taking walks in the evening to the edge of town, where he could observe birds in flight. Encouraged by what he had seen, and feeling confident that man might be able to duplicate the feat, he decided to write the Smithsonian Institution and ask for the best books relating to the subject. The letter he wrote the Smithsonian on May 30, 1899, would set in motion a series of events that would eventually change the world.

Several days later, Wilbur received a package from the Smithsonian containing a number of articles, plus a list of books he might wish to purchase. By now, Orville's interest had been aroused by Wilbur's growing, enthusiastic belief that man could fly. Both brothers read the articles sent by the Smithsonian, then sent off for the recommended books. When the volumes arrived, they were devoured by hungry minds. Two of the books, one by E. C. Huffaker and one by Samuel P. Langley, were of questionable value. One of the books, however, written by Octave Chanute, would have a significant impact.

Aeronautics Gets a Champion

Chanute, a respected civil engineer responsible for building the first bridge across the Missouri River at Kansas City in 1870, had been interested in the problem of aerial navigation since his youth. He had carefully concealed that interest, however, in order to protect his career. The fastest way to be labeled a nut in the latter part of the nineteenth century was to profess a belief in manned flight. People who did suffered ridicule and, very often, loss of employment. It wasn't until Chanute reached his sixties and had achieved a degree of financial independence that he "went public" with his research. In 1894 he published a book, *Progress in Flying Machines,* summarizing the information he had been accumulating. It was a book the Wright brothers would study for a year, reading and rereading passages, discussing and debating theories.

Octave Chanute was confident that the flying problem would be solved, but felt it might take a long time. It had taken the bicycle nearly a decade to evolve from one-wheel monster to the new "safety" bike enjoyed by millions. It would surely take as long—if not longer—to build a successful flying machine. In an article in *McClure's Magazine* in 1900, Chanute suggested it would take a collaboration of individuals to solve the problem, because no man could simultaneously be an inventor, engineer, mathematician, and practical mechanic, not to mention the capitalist needed to furnish or raise funds. Chanute was right; no one man could be all those things. He never dreamed, however, that *two could.* Especially two bicycle mechanics from Dayton, Ohio.

> The fastest way to be labeled a nut in the latter part of the nineteenth century was to profess a belief in manned flight.

Introducing the Masters

"Who invented the airplane?" the question is asked. "The Wright brothers," the answer comes back. Not Wilbur and Orville Wright . . . the *Wright brothers.* We give the men a collective identity because most people cannot find, on the surface, a discernible difference. Their partnership was so effective, so seamless, that we just lump the two together in the generic category of "brothers." The fact that Wilbur and Orville meshed so well in their work, however, does not imply that they were identical. Although the personalities and character of Wilbur and Orville will emerge in greater detail in the illustrations throughout this book, it's useful at this point, by way of introduction, to provide a brief sketch of each. The differences soon become apparent.

For example, although both men habitually dressed in business suits with stiff celluloid collars and ties, Orville really cared about his appearance. He was, in fact, a bit of a dandy. Whereas Wilbur wore his clothes, Orville displayed them, taking care to make sure his clothes were always clean and pressed. In one picture of the two men sitting on the front porch of their home on Hawthorn Street in Dayton, Wilbur, wearing a somewhat rumpled suit, is slouched against the wall. Orville, on the other hand, is sitting ramrod straight (to protect against wrinkling, no doubt) with hands folded over knees. A sharp crease is evident in his trousers, which are pulled up to reveal a natty pair of argyle socks.

Both men were quiet and reserved around outsiders, but often animated and enthusiastic around family. Orville enjoyed playing games, and frequently he was the cause of laughter in Wright family gatherings. Often viewed as serious and lackluster, both brothers were actually witty and humorous. Wright brother biographer Tom Crouch refutes the notion that the men were dull. Having read all their correspondence, Crouch describes the brothers as "warm, interesting, witty, and articulate." They were both, however, highly focused and dedicated to their work. And deeply private.

Little Brother (Orville)

In *Wright Reminiscences,* Ivonette Wright Miller relates a telling story about her "Uncle Orv." Sometime in the 1920s, Orville, who was a fan of Ohio State football, attended a game in Columbus. When a young man came around selling programs, Orville paid for the program with a brand new dollar bill. He was reading the program when the young man returned several minutes later after noticing that Orville had given him two dollars instead of one. "Uncle Orv was so impressed with his honesty," Ivonette wrote, "he asked for his name and address. When he returned home he sent the boy an autographed picture of the first flight." Can you imagine what that's worth today? There was nothing Orville admired more than honesty.

Orville's intense integrity would cast its influence over everything he did. His loyalty to family and friends, his pride of ownership in the work he did, his meticulous attention to detail—all were the product of his strong commitment to integrity and honesty. This by no means implies that Orville was a stuffy do-gooder. Despite painful shyness with strangers, Orville was known within his family as a fun-loving man who took pleasure in playing friendly practical jokes. Once, at dinner, he placed a small mechanical cockroach under an overturned plate in front of a nephew. When the boy turned the plate over, Orville tugged on a thread he had attached to the mechanical insect, making it jump. And everyone else, too! When you read the remembrances of Orville written by those closest to him, words like "warm," "gracious," and "fun loving" come up repeatedly.

Like his brother, Orville was modest and gracious. He was always, one friend noted, the last man to pass through a door. His thoughtfulness and kind demeanor, however, masked an intense desire to challenge and improve everything around him. Ivonette Miller says her uncle was always bubbling over with ideas. Miller recalls Orville as a "dreamer and idealist quick to see why things didn't work and full of ideas as to how he could improve their efficiency." His curiosity and appetite for solving problems would be just as intense in the last days of his life as they had been on the sandy slopes of Kill Devil Hills.

Orville was the more upbeat of the two brothers. During a particularly difficult time in 1901, when a discouraged Wilbur wanted to throw in the towel and quit, it was Orville's positive attitude that pulled his brother back to work on the problem. Orville's skills were considerable. He was a master mechanic and craftsman who took pride in being precise and exact in his work. Although not as conceptual as Wilbur, he was the better mathematician. He could convert almost anything on paper into a tangible reality. Many times, as they hammered out the details of their flying machine, Wilbur would describe to Orville what was needed. Orville would then produce the exact item described.

Big Brother (Wilbur)

Much has been written about Wilbur Wright, but occasionally researchers find something that allows them to look past the blurry picture that history often paints of its heroes. Ivonette Miller shares such a story about her "Uncle Will." When Wilbur went to France in 1908, he was invited to work on and store his flying machine at the automobile manufacturing plant of Léon Bolleé. While there, Wilbur did something that captured the hearts of the other workmen: He arrived and departed when they did. "He kept the same hours the others did," Miller writes, "and his whole behavior was as if he were simply one more workman." When the whistle blew for lunch, Wilbur, dressed in overalls, grabbed his lunch pail and ate with the men. The workers were overwhelmed that one of the most famous people in the world, the man who had conquered the sky, would want to take his meals with them. Wilbur, I'm sure, never gave the matter any thought.

The mental picture of Wilbur in overalls carrying a lunch pail doesn't quite jibe with the image often conveyed of him as the genius and driving force behind the *Wright Flyer.* It was Wilbur who was first interested in the flying problem, later drawing Orville into the challenge. It was Wilbur who got things rolling with letters to the Smithsonian Institution and to aviation expert Octave Chanute in Chicago. Although both brothers were good writers, Wilbur had the greater skill. It was decided early that Wilbur would take the lead in recording their progress. Despite feeling uncomfortable around strangers, Wilbur was a highly competent speaker. When a presentation was required of the Wright brothers, Wilbur made it.

Wilbur often comes off as dour and solemn in many of his public appearances. Although not as shy as his younger brother, he by no means craved the public limelight. But he possessed a wry sense of humor that would emerge from time to time in his public engagements. Once, when accepting an award, he was asked why his comments were so short. "The most talkative bird in the world is a parrot," he replied, "but he is a poor flier!" On another occasion, when asked about the absence of a mate, he responded, "I don't have time for a wife *and* an airplane!" Wilbur Wright was one of those unique men who drew others to him by the power of his presence, a power that did not need words to convey it.

While both men possessed a strong intellect, Wilbur was the more disciplined thinker. An avid reader, Wilbur devoured the books in his father's library on history, theology, literature, and science. He enjoyed the novels of Sir Walter Scott, but *Plutarch's Lives* was his favorite book. Extremely analytical, Wilbur had the ability to view a problem in his mind three-dimensionally. Like the computer-aided design systems that allow today's designers the option of rotating drawings on a computer screen, Wilbur could do the same in his mind. He had the mind and aptitude of an engineer and scientist.

An Incredible Story

The writer trying to tell the story of Wilbur and Orville Wright encounters one major obstacle right at the beginning: The tale seems to straddle the fence between nonfiction and fiction, leaning precariously toward the latter. Here's the greatest problem of the age, one so complicated no one on the planet had been able to solve it, yet two men who had accomplished little of note and made their way in life patching inner tubes and "peddling" bicycles (no pun intended) somehow got it together and conceptually solved the problem in eleven months.

In ten short years, they went from accepting orders for bicycle parts to accepting medals from kings.

And they only worked on it part-time. You begin to feel somewhere along the line that you've gone from being a reporter of history to a creator of fiction. And not very believable fiction at that.

Nevertheless, the story is true. Wilbur and Orville Wright, the third and fourth sons of an itinerant preacher, went from relative obscurity to international acclaim in less than a decade. In ten short years, they went from accepting orders for bicycle parts to accepting medals from kings. Heads of state would scramble to have their pictures taken with the men; presidents would seek their endorsement. It's an incredible story, one that is at once wonderfully inspiring and terribly puzzling. One that leads virtually every reader to ask the same question: How did they do it? How did two bicycle builders from America's heartland manage to do what the best and brightest scientists in the world could not?

Many books have been written in an attempt to answer that question. Some, written for the juvenile market as "morality tales," attribute the brothers' success to strong character traits: integrity, ingenuity, perseverance, and so on. Those traits, of course, have to be considered, since the personalities and makeup of the men were certainly a factor. Other books, written for the adult reader, probe deeper into their work, attributing their success to everything from sheer genius to the methodical application of the scientific method and engineering principles. Still others have looked into the remarkable Wright family history for "genetic" clues.

If these sundry reasons for their success were presented to the reader as a multiple-choice question, the correct answer would be "all of the above," and then some. The truth is, there is no one factor that led to their success. It was a unique, perhaps one-time occurrence when opportunity and preparedness, like two trains on the same track, collided to make something big happen. One part of the story containing an important piece of the puzzle hasn't been properly emphasized, however.

As noted, many of the books written about the Wright brothers were written for children to impart lessons on character and morality. Work hard, study your lessons, respect others, stay curious—and you will make a success of yourself. The Wright story, as directed to children, was meant not only to inspire, but to be *learned from*. That's what has been missing in adult versions of the story. There are lessons to be learned from the Wright brothers that are ready to impact a *whole new demographic:* leaders and managers charged with building teams, solving problems, and taking their performance to another level.

Principles for Business Today

The one aspect of the Wright brothers' story that has yet to be told is that a key component of their problem-solving process was the application of a set of identifiable principles. Although these principles were never recorded by the brothers, it's easy to see, upon close examination of their inventive process, that they were there. Guidelines, many with origins in the personalities and values of the brothers, emerge as pieces of a model that directed their action and behavior. The skills the Wright brothers were acquiring in the back room of their bicycle shop would one day coalesce into a practical strategy for inventing a flying machine.

Although different in so many respects, the men were remarkably compatible. They complemented each other, each providing a skill or discipline the other lacked. Working side-by-side, the

> They learned to work in concert with one another, developing a level of confidence and trust they would be willing to bet their lives on.

brothers developed a relationship I like to call Team Wright. They learned to work in concert with one another, developing a level of confidence and trust they would be willing to bet their lives on. The teamwork that evolved would one day be admired for its seamless function and remarkable equity. In fact, it becomes a problem-solving principle in itself.

Other skills would emerge as well, skills that would eventually comprise an effective and efficient problem-solving model. In the years the brothers were partners in business, first as printers, then as bicycle builders, they would acquire or refine:

- A passion for knowledge and information

- An ability to argue through tough issues in search of truth

- An ability to identify the hardest part of a problem, and the discipline to begin there

- A talent for tactile and conceptual tinkering

- An ability to conceptualize new (often radical) ideas, and the courage to consider them

- A penchant for method and meticulous attention to detail

- An ability to create infinitely more together than they could by themselves

The brothers were refining the skills—mechanical and conceptual—they would need to solve the problem of heavier-than-air manned flight. Skills, relevant and viable, that comprise a problem-solving model I call . . . *The Wright Way*.

The Wright Way

In studying the history of aviation, it becomes apparent that many experimenters were approaching the heavier-than-air flying problem in dramatically different fashion. Those attacking the problem ranged in sophistication from barnyard mechanics to learned men decked out in doctoral robes. Theories on manned flight would be just as varied. Some believed the answer to the problem lay in generating sufficient power for propulsion; others believed in developing control and balance. Some, disregarding the laws of physics, thought the answer lay in getting small models to fly, then simply "scaling them up." Approaches ran from the intuitive (the seat-of-the-pants approach) to the scientific. Only one worked, however, and that was *The Wright Way*.

A number of Wright brother biographers, most notably Tom Crouch and Peter Jakab, have made the case that Wilbur and Orville solved the problem of heavier-than-air powered flight by the systematic application of engineering principles. Although neither of the Wright brothers had formal training or education in engineering or technology, both Crouch and Jakab attribute a strong "engineering influence" to the brothers' success. I tend to agree, especially as it applies to technology issues. The premise of *The Wright Way* is not to question or supplant the solved-as-engineers theory, but to augment it with a more general problem-solving model.

The Wright Way is a set of seven problem-solving principles culled from the extraordinary accomplishments of Wilbur and Orville Wright, who achieved an "impossible" goal when they discovered the solution to manned flight. These are not technical principles that will enable you to understand the concept of three-axis navigation or calculate angle of incidence. These are the precepts that guided the Wright brothers as they sought to understand, then resolve, those technical questions. These are the principles Wilbur and Orville Wright used a hundred years ago that are just as relevant today. These principles, if applied to your business or organization, will not just get it off the ground, they will make it soar!

CHAPTER ONE

THE EVENT OF THE CENTURY

"To invent an airplane is nothing. To build one is something. But to fly is everything."

Otto Lilienthal (1848–1896), aviation pioneer

IT WAS an odd assortment of men that made the four-mile trek from "Camp Wright" over to Kitty Hawk. One, a lumber dealer from Manteo, had come over to search the rugged Atlantic coast for debris from a recent shipwreck. Hearing talk about a couple of guys who were planning to fly, he had hung around to "see the show." Three others were surfmen from the Kill Devil Hills Lifesaving Station, grizzled veterans of the sea who had befriended the two "odd ducks" from Dayton. The last member of the group was the seventeen-year-old son of a Nags Head widow who made her way in life telling the fortunes of vacationers for "twenty-five cents a go." Despite their considerable differences, the men had come together that day to form a historic team: the world's first aircraft ground crew. Answering the summons of the Wright brothers to assist them on the morning of December 17, 1903, they had just witnessed the brothers' leap into the pages of history.

The Death of Impossibility

Having assisted the Wright brothers in their fourth and final flight of the day (an unexpected gust of wind crumbled the delicate flying machine before more attempts could be made), the men were hiking over to Kitty Hawk to share the news. Hearty souls accustomed to solitude, one might assume they walked in silence, contemplating what they had just seen. John Daniels, a strapping young seaman charged by Orville with the responsibility of taking the official photograph of the flight, may have wondered if he'd tripped the shutter in time to capture the moment. Years later, Daniels would be credited with snapping the most famous photograph in aviation history. It was the only picture he would ever take.

Bill Tate, a key figure in the Wright brothers' story at Kitty Hawk, should have been there to see the flight. On the morning of the 17th, Tate stepped outside his home at Martins Point and felt the bite of a Cape Hatteras sting-wind. That wind, combined with the patches of ice forming on the puddles in his yard, convinced Tate that there would be no attempt at flying that day. Later in the morning he changed his mind and decided to make the trip over to Kitty Hawk. Near the post office, Tate saw a small band of men heading his way. As the group neared, Johnny Moore, the fortune-teller's son, couldn't resist telling him of the Wright brothers' good fortune. Moore broke into a wild run hollering, "They done it! They done it! Damn'd if they ain't flew!" Tate was heartsick. Missing the Wright brothers' first flight would be the regret of his life.

Back at the campsite, having just accomplished what man had dreamed of doing since the dawn of civilization, Wilbur and Orville returned to their shelter to warm themselves and enjoy a leisurely meal. They may have just flown, but they were still hungry. Later, eyewitnesses would recall that the brothers didn't seem particularly enthused or excited about what they had accomplished. Perhaps the bitter cold had numbed their excitement. Maybe the first flight adrenaline rush had worn off, subduing their spirits. Or maybe they had *expected* to fly all along. They were, after all, used to solving problems.

A Staggering Event Worn Smooth

Time has a way of taking the edge off things. If the achievement of the Wright brothers seems any less profound today than when Johnny Moore first shouted the news, it's only because its edges have been worn smooth with familiarity. After the Wrights, new ideas and inventions poured forth in such a torrent that the identities of the creators were often lost in the flood. In many respects, the Wright brothers were the first and last "celebrity" inventors of the twentieth century. Today, few people can tell us who invented the microchip or laser, or even television for that matter. We fax messages and make copies daily, yet we have no idea who the creative genius behind each invention was. Combine this with the fact that we've lost our ability to be truly amazed by just about anything, and you can see why the magnitude of what Wilbur and Orville Wright accomplished may have been diminished.

It would be like Neil Armstrong landing on the moon in a craft he had built himself and paid for with a part-time job.

When the Wright brothers solved the problem of heavier-than-air flight, they not only achieved a technological breakthrough, they stunned the world. It was an incredible achievement with no modern parallel. The only thing that might come close would be if Neil Armstrong had landed on the moon in a craft he had built himself and paid for with a part-time job. To put it into context, consider this: The big news item in the papers the day Wilbur and Orville conquered the air was the story of Colonel H. Nelson Jackson, who, in order to win a fifty-dollar bet, had driven cross-country in an automobile in the unheard-of time of just *sixty-three days!* The Wright brothers' invention would one day extract 99.8 percent of the time needed to make Nelson's journey. Wilbur and Orville had redefined the world's concept of time and distance.

Unacknowledged Heroes

What the Wright brothers accomplished at Kill Devil Hills that December day in 1903 would cast a shadow of influence over the entire twentieth century. It was so staggering that many people—including aviation experts—refused to believe it had occurred. "Their success came so suddenly and from such an unexpected quarter," says historian Gary

Bradshaw, "that their contemporaries could not believe they had done what they claimed." Aeronautical circles were not easily persuaded, and in the era of William Randolph Hearst, newspapers were not entirely trusted. Five years after the first flight, the majority of Americans refused to acknowledge the feat, even when confronted with pictures in a newspaper. "The public, discouraged by failure and tragedies just witnessed," Wilbur later commented, "considered flight beyond the reach of man." Or, as Wright biographer John McMahon expressed it, "The world believed less in the airplane than the sea serpent."

People not only regarded heavier-than-air flight as out of reach, they felt that those who tried it were deserving of ridicule. Samuel Pierpont Langley, the respected secretary of the Smithsonian Institution, who had two embarrassing plunges into the Potomac River to show for his efforts, was hounded by the media. The *Boston Herald* cruelly suggested that Langley should concentrate his efforts on submarines, not flying machines. An editorial in *The New York Times* written after Langley's second failure on December 8, 1903, predicted that manned flight was achievable, but only if scientists and mathematicians worked on it around-the-clock for the next "one to ten million years." It wouldn't take ten million years. It wouldn't even take ten days.

The Giants Had Quit

When Wilbur and Orville took on the challenge of manned flight, it was at a time when most people, including those who had worked on it the longest and hardest, had given up. Making the achievement all the more remarkable was the stature of those who had tried and failed. Alexander Graham Bell couldn't figure it out. Thomas Edison, whose dogged persistence (thousands of failures before success) in developing the incandescent lightbulb was the stuff of legend, gave up on this one. Hiram Maxim, the inventor of the Maxim rapid-fire gun, spent $200,000 on the problem before calling it quits. These were the lucky ones. Pioneers like Otto Lilienthal, Percy Pilcher, and John Montgomery paid for the privilege of challenging the skies with their lives.

The Wright brothers had methodically and meticulously worked their way through the problem of heavier-than-air, powered and controlled flight, and solved it. The actual flight of Orville wasn't as much the answer to the problem as it was a confirmation of the process used to achieve it. In solving the problem, the Wright brothers resolved hundreds of smaller challenges that, when taken as a whole, yielded the first flight. For the brothers, the solution to the flying problem was actually a systematic process guided by an established, if not written, set of principles. The first flight was the culmination of that process. That's why the brothers weren't particularly excited or enthused when it occurred. For Wilbur and Orville, the first flight was just another step along a problem-solving continuum.

A Problem of Enormous Complexity

It is impossible to overstate what the Wright brothers accomplished. Bill Gates, founder and CEO of Microsoft Corp., calls the first flight "the single greatest cultural force since the invention of writing." Harry Combs, author of *Kill Devil Hill: Discovering the Secret of the Wright Brothers,* says the achievement "rattled the planet" and places its importance on a par with man's discovery of the use of fire. Like these people and many others, I believe Wilbur and Orville's achievement deserves recognition as *the event* of the twentieth century. If I were an attorney charged with making the case for the brothers, here's the evidence I'd place before the court:

● *They solved an "unsolvable" problem.* The idea of man flying was accepted, as Wilbur and Orville would later note, as the "standard of impossibility" in 1900. A popular phrase of the day went as follows: "If God had meant for man to fly, feathers would be sprouting on his shoulders!" Lord Kelvin, a highly regarded scientist and president of the Royal Society of London, stated flatly in 1885, "Heavier-than-air flying machines are impossible." By the turn of the century, many of those who had

> Their flying machine was the product of their own hands, and it was assembled as if their lives depended on it, which they did.

been working on the problem for years had thrown in the towel. "The mystery," Combs wrote, "had been lethal in defense of its secrets." The Wright brothers solved a highly complex, technical problem the best and brightest of the day had deemed unsolvable.

➻ *They launched the era of aviation.* Although people give credit to the Wright brothers for inventing the world's first heavier-than-air flying machine, few realize that Wilbur and Orville invented the science of flight as well. As Wilbur later noted, there was no art of flying when they began, just a "flying problem." There was no pilot's manual in 1903 to guide the men as they eased their flyer into the cold December sky. They literally wrote the book as they went. Many critical elements of flight in use today were originated by the Wright brothers a hundred years ago.

➻ *They did it all, with no subcontracting.* The achievement of the Wright brothers is made all the more remarkable by the fact that they did everything themselves. They conducted the research, framed the problem, and formulated the strategies to solve it. If they needed a part, they made it. If they didn't have the tools needed to make the part, they made the tools. Their flying machine was the product of their own hands, and it was assembled as if their lives depended on it, which they did. The flying machines of Wilbur and Orville Wright bore their finger-prints alone. "The Wright brothers," says Tom Crouch in *The Bishop's Boys,* "were the inventors of the airplane in a stricter sense than Edison the lightbulb, Ford the automobile, or Bell the telephone."

➻ *They did it with amazing speed.* Despite the fact that man had been working on the problem of manned flight for centuries (drawings indicate Leonardo da Vinci was playing around with the idea in 1485), no one was close to the solution when the Wright brothers took up the challenge in May 1899. They solved the problem in an astonishing period of just fifty-five months, working on it part-time! Even more amazing is the fact that they had actually worked out the answer two years before their his-toric flight. After a winter of intense research in 1901, Wilbur and Orville knew they had the theoretical solution to manned flight in hand. The rest of the time would be spent learning to actually fly.

➡ *They did it with little formal training or education.* Pictures of Professor Samuel Pierpont Langley, the leading candidate in the race to fly in 1900, often showed the noted scientist decked out in his doctoral robes. As head of the Smithsonian Institution, the most prestigious scientific post in America, Langley held a position that demanded academic credentials. Most of those who attacked the problem of heavier-than-air, powered flight at the turn of the century were trained or degreed scientists and engineers. Neither of the Wright brothers, in terms of formal education, had as much as a high school diploma. They were self-taught aviators.

➡ *They "shrank" the world.* The Wright brothers redefined time and distance in the twentieth century. As a result of their efforts, the world would have both a new intimacy and a new urgency. The Wright brothers allowed people to think in terms of hours, not days, as they considered transportation options. Along with Alexander Graham Bell and Henry Ford, the Wright brothers were major contributors to the death of distance in the United States.

➡ *They achieved an extraordinary ROI (return on investment).* Although others had offered to finance their research, Wilbur and Orville were concerned that accepting outside funds might result in a loss of control over their work. Drawing on profits from their bicycle business, the cumulative amount spent by the Wrights in developing their flying machine would be less than $1,000. By comparison, the launch mechanism alone for Langley's flying machine cost $50,000. Hiram Maxim spent more than $200,000 on his efforts. Clément Ader, a French flying-machine pioneer, raised $100,000 in government funding and spent it all before giving up. The Wright brothers' invention was one of the great returns on investment in history.

➡ *They broke a significant psychological bond.* As paradigm shifts go, the accomplishments of Wilbur and Orville Wright ushered in one of the greatest. They not only solved a seemingly unsolvable problem, they broke a significant psychological bond, one that said man was bound to earth. No longer criticized or disdained for their "crazy ideas," creative thinkers and inventors world-wide were free—even encouraged—to pursue the "impossible." After the Wright brothers, even the sky was no longer the limit.

↝ *They had global impact.* Many of the earliest (and best) pho-tographs of the Wright brothers in flight were taken in Europe, where Wilbur and Orville made demonstration flights. Frustrated with the U.S. military's lack of interest, the brothers took their flying machine overseas, where they were acclaimed as conquer-ing heroes. It wasn't until 1908, five years after the first flight, that many Americans would see what Europe had seen. The U.S. government's failure to respond to the brothers' achievement had spawned the globalization of flight, leading to economic, cul-tural, and geopolitical changes worldwide.

↝ *They altered the economy.* The rapid transport of people and material across great distances became a reality because of the Wright brothers. They altered the future of many industries and created others. It wasn't long before the rail-roads began to feel the shadow of the *Wright Flyer* falling across their future. New indus-tries—commercial, military, and leisure—would be created as a result. One of the first government agencies to take advantage of the Wright brothers' invention wasn't the military but the post office, which began airmail ser-vice in 1911 on Long Island. The first airmail stamps cost twenty-four cents, a lot of money at the time.

> **Orville's injuries—a shattered hip, fractured ribs and tibia, scalp wounds, and concussion—would cause him pain the rest of his life.**

↝ *They restored brainpower as a force majeure.* The brothers devel-oped the world's first heavier-than-air flying machine not by building on an existing body of research, but by setting it aside. Inventors such as Ford, Bell, and Morse had the luxury of building on the work of previous researchers. The Wright broth-ers, on the other hand, ended up having to reject the "known truth" about flying to get at the solution. They were the first aviation pioneers to seriously think the whole problem through. It was a reminder to a world enamored with machines that brainpower was at least as important as horsepower in making things happen.

➤ *They put their personal safety on the line.* Unlike those inventors who were able to conduct their research in a laboratory, Wilbur and Orville had to take to the skies to perfect their invention—the same skies that would claim the lives of Lilienthal, Pilcher, and Montgomery. In 1908, while trying to qualify his flyer for the military, Orville took Lieutenant Thomas Selfridge up with him as a passenger. While aloft, a propeller splintered, severing a guy wire to the rudder. The machine spun out of control and crashed to the ground in seconds. Orville's injuries—a shattered hip, fractured ribs and tibia, scalp wounds, and concussion—would cause him pain the rest of his life. Selfridge, on the other hand, would make history. He became the world's first casualty from an airplane crash.

In terms of its capacity to inspire, few accomplishments can match what these modest bicycle mechanics from Dayton achieved. Orville Wright's twelve-second journey, which took place in near obscurity, would become man's most visible evidence to date that the impossible was not out of mankind's reach. The first flight not only redefined our world, it redefined the human spirit. It was not a quirk of fate.

Problem-Solving Nuggets

The untapped vein of gold for the business reader is that the Wright brothers followed a set of problem-solving principles that can be used today. These principles were never recorded or discussed by the brothers. After inventing the flying machine, Wilbur and Orville did not set out on a national tour to present problem-solving workshops and seminars to business leaders and managers. As you read their words and study their work, you will not see references to terms like "forging" or phrases like "tackle the tyrant." I've created those terms to make it easier to grasp and retain the principles they reveal. What you will see, however, are many

examples of how the brothers applied these principles in unraveling the
mysteries of flight.

The Wright Way

It's not unusual for people, in fixating on the actual thing created, to miss
an equally important accomplishment. Henry Ford is often acknowledged
(incorrectly) as the inventor of the automobile while his greatest achievement, the manufacturing assembly line, goes unmentioned. Although the
automobile was certainly important, it was the assembly line that revolutionized America. In many respects, the same thing is true of the Wright
brothers. As the nation celebrates the one-hundredth anniversary of the
first flight, it is hailing the creation of the flying machine while ignoring
the part most useful to business today: the process that created it.

The objective of *The Wright Way* is to present, in straightforward and
easy-to-understand fashion, seven key principles that Wilbur and Orville
Wright used to solve the problem of heavier-than-air manned flight. The
seven principles are:

Forging	The principle of constructive conflict
Tackling the tyrant	The principle of worst things first
Fiddling	The principle of inveterate tinkering
Mind-warping	The principle of rigid flexibility
Relentless preparation	The principle of forever learning
Measuring twice	The principle of methodical meticulousness
Force multiplication	The principle of equitable teamwork

These principles, each of which is fully explained and illustrated in a
separate chapter, will give the reader enough ideas (and creative energy)
to dislodge even the most stubborn of problems and exploit the most difficult of challenges.

The Problem They Solved

Sir George Cayley, an English aerial scientist in the early nineteenth century, is often credited with being the first person to correctly frame the flying problem. The problem, as Cayley accurately noted, was to "make a surface support a given weight by the application of power to the resistance of air." More simply stated, the problem of flight is to make air support a heavier-than-air flying machine by the resistance created when it's propelled through the air. Correctly defining the problem of heavier-than-air flight is important not only in understanding it, but in making sure that those who solved it—Wilbur and Orville Wright—get the proper credit. It's equally important in discrediting the claims of others.

The key element in determining who really solved the problem lies in how you define the concept of flying. If "flying" means getting a craft off the ground and into the air, then there are a number of gliding pioneers who could claim that honor. If it means taking what aviation historian Charles Gibbs-Smith calls a "short hop" in a powered machine, then Hiram Maxim or Clément Ader might be accorded first-flight honors. Short hops and long glides come well short of the established criteria for determining a successful flight, however. As enumerated by Gibbs-Smith, the criteria include:

- That the machine be a heavier-than-air craft (no balloons or dirigibles)

- That the operator (i.e., pilot) be able to control it on three axes (pitch, roll, and yaw)

- That the machine be powered by some sort of engine

- That the machine take off from level ground under its own power

- That the machine be able to sustain itself in flight

- That the machine be able to return safely to the ground

If these requirements constitute the accepted definition of heavier-than-air flight, the only people who can lay claim to being the first to "fly" are the Wright brothers. They alone met all six criteria.

The story of the Wright brothers' triumph at Kill Devil Hills in December 1903 is the story of two men approaching an incredibly complex problem methodically and strategically. As history, it captures a remarkable period in America's past, a time when the country's self-image was forever altered. Americans were asking at the dawn of a new century, "If we can fly, what *can't* we do?" As a technical read, the story is a fascinating look at the process of invention. Even if you don't understand concepts such as pitch, roll, and yaw, the tale is worth pursuing. The saga of the Wright brothers is a powerful and inspiring story of family, dedication, opportunity, discouragement, perseverance, and, ultimately, triumph.

Solving Problems Is What We Do

In Sir Arthur Conan Doyle's *The Red-Headed League,* Sherlock Holmes comments: "It's quite a three-pipe problem, and I beg that you won't speak to me for fifty minutes!" It would be nice if we could all solve our problems in fifty minutes or less. Sherlock notwithstanding, most of us require more time. We may require much more time if we have a predilection for avoiding the process altogether. One of my favorite cartoons features a man sitting at his desk with a deer-caught-in-the-headlamps look on his face. He punches the button on his intercom and asks his administrative assistant, "Miss Jones, could you bring me a simple, obvious problem to solve?"

Most of us can commiserate with this guy. It seems that our days are filled with an endless parade of difficulties that demand our attention. Sometimes my day reminds me of a definition I heard years ago in a Franklin Planner seminar. "Time," the leader said, "is what keeps one thing after another from being every damn thing all at once." Many of us approach our problems with a negative perspective. The logic seems to be that a problem is something to be dealt with, so that we can go on to more productive things. It's a mind-set that not only robs us of enjoyment, it can obscure the one thing essential to the success of any organization: opportunities.

Solving problems is what businesspeople do even if they dread the process, which they shouldn't. Charles Kettering, another famous Daytonian, once told his staff, "Don't bring me anything but trouble . . . good news weakens me!" Most people probably think Kettering was a nut. But the fact of the matter is, he conditioned himself to view problems as opportunities. If a business cannot solve problems, it cannot exist. Indeed, it would not deserve to. On the most elementary level, solving the problems of customers is a business's raison d'être . . . its reason for existence. If the product a company or organization produces does not solve someone's problem (i.e., need, want, or desire), it does not in reality have a product. And that's a real problem!

Most of us are conditioned to view problems as something to be minimized, if not avoided altogether. Few of us are able to see problems as opportunities to soar, especially when they start piling up. The Encarta dictionary defines a problem as "a question or puzzle to be solved." Unfortunately, when you introduce the extraneous factors—angry customers, demanding bosses, undermotivated workers, etc.—that puzzle or question takes on quite a different appearance. You may be saying, "Let the Wright brothers take on lagging sales, missed shipping dates, or high employee turnover, and see how they do." I think they would do quite well, because they would have a problem-solving model for addressing those issues.

Steps Versus Principles

There's a difference between problem-solving steps and problem-solving principles. Defining a problem, gathering information, and selecting the best option are problem-solving steps learned in business school. They provide the structure needed to correctly frame the problem, then guide the person attacking the problem through the process. Problem-solving steps work best on what are referred to as algorithmic problems. In other words, there is some sort of procedure to guide the problem solver.

In an economy that operates at the "speed of blur," the Wright brothers' model is all the more desirable.

When I was teaching personnel supervision at Indiana University several years ago, I taught my students the Hot Stove Rule of employee discipline. The concept was that, through a set number of steps that gradually turned up the heat on a problem worker, the worker would be motivated to perform as desired. If the employee still didn't perform as desired, the supervisor would, at least, have the documentation needed to terminate him. This was an algorithmic problem solved by following set steps.

Most of the problems managers and leaders face today are less definitive. They are more heuristic in nature, requiring something more than just following predetermined steps. These are the problems where no set procedure exists. These are the problems resolved by the thinking power and creative ability of their attackers. The ability to resolve them is enhanced by the ability to combine natural skills with solid principles to formulate a problem-solving model. That's what this book is all about.

There are many practical benefits to be gained from the problem-solving principles of the Wright brothers, but none greater than these: They save time and they save money. In an economy that operates at the "speed of blur," the Wright brothers' model is all the more desirable. By attacking the key parts first, eliminating costly errors and backtracks, and surfacing creative options, the brothers solved the problem of flight in what, at the time, was mind-boggling speed. The fact that the principles they followed minimized their costs (less than $1,000) is an added bonus. If speed to market and return on investment are important to your business, these principles are priceless.

CHAPTER TWO

MASTERS OF THE PROBLEM

By far the greatest obstacle to the progress of science and to the understanding of new tasks and provinces therein is found in this—that men despair and think things impossible.

Francis Bacon (1561–1624),
Lord Chancellor of England

SIMON NEWCOMB was not among those who gathered along the Potomac River on October 7, 1903, to witness Professor Samuel Langley's first attempt at manned flight. Newcomb, the only American since Benjamin Franklin to be made an associate of the prestigious Institute of France, was one of America's most gifted and honored scientists. He was a renowned Johns Hopkins mathematician, a savvy physicist, and a giant in the field of celestial mechanics. In his "spare time," Newcomb was one of the economists responsible for developing the Quantity Theory of Money. Albert Einstein would later acknowledge the importance of Newcomb's work in the development of his Theory of Relativity.

It's surprising that Newcomb, as one of the "giants of discovery" at the dawn of the twentieth century, would pass on the opportunity to witness history in the making. Even more so since Langley was involved. Dr. Langley was secretary of the Smithsonian Institution, the most prestigious scientific post in America. His exalted stature had enabled him to secure the backing of both the Smithsonian and the United States military to fund his effort to invent a heavier-than-air flying machine. Nevertheless, on the day Langley's machine, called the *Great Aerodrome,* was put to the test, Simon Newcomb had better things to do. He "took a pass" on the event because he knew, beyond a shadow of doubt, it would fail.

Several weeks after the *Great Aerodrome* had "fallen like a sack of mortar" (one reporter's description) into the Potomac, Newcomb wrote an article for *The Independent* explaining why it had done so. In it, he not only refuted the possibility of manned flight, he detailed what would happen should anyone succeed in getting a flying machine in the air. With palpable arrogance, Newcomb stated, "Once he (the pilot) slackens his speed, he'll fall out of the sky!" If such a scientific luminary as Simon Newcomb thought flight was impossible, how could anyone justify taking on the problem? Especially two bicycle mechanics from Dayton, Ohio.

The Big Question

Read any book on the Wright brothers and it won't be long before you encounter a question similar to the one Peter Jakab puts forth in *Visions of a Flying Machine.* Jakab asks:

> How were these two men, working essentially alone, with little formal scientific or technical training, able to solve a problem so complex and demanding as heavier-than-air flight in only a few short years, when it had defied better known experimenters for centuries?

Wright biographers and aviation experts have grappled for decades to find an adequate response to the question. It seems inconceivable that a problem of such complexity could be solved by such unlikely candidates.

To find the answer, or as much of it as is possible, the researcher has to do his homework. On the surface, we see two Midwestern mechanics tinkering around in the back shed. When we dig deeper, we find two precise and careful men who worked out complicated mathematical formulas to create lift tables accurate a hundred years later. On the surface, we see two brothers sitting on their front porch, "hashing things out" after dinner. When we dig deeper, we discover two disciplined and analytical minds working methodically through the problem. The answer, it seems, lies below the surface.

Why the question is even asked needs to be considered as much as the question. Although it's hard to separate Wilbur and Orville from the issue, I believe part of the reason for asking lies outside of the brothers themselves. The origin of the question, in my opinion, is split evenly among three factors: the enormity of the problem, the obscurity of its occurrence, and the campaign by the Smithsonian Institution afterward to discredit the achievement. Since each of these holds a piece of the puzzle, a quick glance will help bring things into focus.

The Enormity of the Problem

The Wright brothers knew, in taking up the flying problem, that they were entering intellectually forbidden territory. To say one intended to fly was to taunt the very laws of gravity. "We knew at the time," Orville commented later, "that flying was the acceptable standard of impossibility." It was, in reality, way past that. People put the possibility of manned flight on a par with perpetual motion. If the problem *were* ever solved, the reasoning went, it would not be the work of "lesser gods." If America's inventive superheroes could not figure it out, whoever did would have to possess skills more advanced than theirs. In the beginning, even the Wright brothers didn't see themselves as viable candidates to solve it.

> The Wright brothers knew, in taking up the flying problem, that they were entering intellectually forbidden territory.

When Wilbur and Orville first considered heavier-than-air manned flight, they looked at it with a certain degree of awe. "Contrary to our previous position," Wilbur later wrote, "we found that men of the very highest standing in the profession of science and invention had attempted to solve the problem. But one by one, they had been compelled to confess themselves beaten." In a letter to the Smithsonian Institution requesting information on aeronautical research, Wilbur noted his goal. "I wish to avail myself of all that is already known and then if possible add my mite to help on the future worker who will attain final success." At that point, Wilbur only expected to push the problem along a bit, not actually solve it.

Relative Obscurity

Although members of their immediate family and a few close friends knew the brothers were working on a flying machine, most Daytonians were unaware that a couple of its sons were seriously pursuing the solution to heavier-than-air manned flight. When it was announced that the Wright brothers had succeeded, the most common response was either doubt or downright disbelief. It was difficult for Daytonians to make the conceptual leap from "Yes, we have your inner tube in stock," to "By the way, we're the first people in history to fly." From an obscurity standpoint, however, that was just the beginning.

One of the more common questions asked about the Wright brothers is why they chose to conduct their research in North Carolina's Outer Banks in the first place. When the Wright brothers began their glider experiments in 1900, they needed four things: steady winds for lift, big hills for takeoffs, soft sand for safe landings, and open space for low-level flying. A fifth, but equally important, need was privacy. Octave Chanute, an aviation pioneer and early Wright brothers' mentor, had conducted his experiments at Indiana Dunes along the shores of Lake Michigan. Although he had an abundance of wind and dunes, he did not have the privacy a remote area like Kill Devil Hills provided. Chanute was besieged by reporters, curiosity seekers, and competitors wishing to "observe" his progress.

The brothers further obscured their work when they returned to Dayton after their successful flights at Kill Devil Hills. Because of concerns over their as-yet-unapproved patent application, the brothers were

It would be 1908, five years after Orville's first flight, before anyone would see a public demonstration of the Wright brothers' flying machine.

reluctant to show their flyer in public. They began conducting tests at Huffman Prairie, a relatively secluded cow pasture just outside of Dayton, but kept publicity to a minimum. They even went so far as to paint the struts on the wings of their flyer gray, to prevent anyone taking a picture from being able to get much in the way of detail. It would be 1908, five years after Orville's first flight, before any-one would see a public demonstration of the Wright brothers' flying machine in America.

After Wilbur's tragic death in 1912 from typhoid fever, Orville sold the company and pursued a life of tinkering in his lab and workshop in downtown Dayton. The records from their work—photographic nega-tives, notebooks and journals, correspondence—were kept from the pub-lic's view. Fred Kelly, the only Wright brother biographer authorized by Orville to tell the story, had access to some of the records, but not all. It wasn't until 1953, five years after Orville's death, that the papers were released. It was only after researchers got a look at the papers and saw the meticulous detail of their experiments that the public realized the com-plete scope of their extraordinary work.

The Smithsonian Affair

The feud between the Smithsonian Institution and the Wright brothers constitutes one of the more bizarre chapters in the history of aviation, and it takes a bit longer to explain. Samuel Langley, the head of the Smithsonian, had been working on the problem of heavier-than-air manned flight for over a decade. A good portion of that time was spent building large mod-els, some with steam- and gas-powered engines, which were successfully flown in tests. By the end of 1903, he had completed a full-size version he called the *Great Aerodrome,* which he was now ready to fly.

The pressure on Langley to be the first to fly was enormous. He not only had the reputation of the Smithsonian to uphold, he had a contract to fill with an increasingly impatient War Department. To say he failed is an understatement. On both attempts to fly (October 7 and December 8, 1903), his *Great Aerodrome* collapsed immediately upon launch from a floating platform. The failures were both public and dramatic. It was a blow to Langley's personal reputation, as well as the prestige of the Smithsonian. Amid growing criticism and ridicule, he resigned his position.

The Wright brothers' success nine days after his failed second attempt at flight probably helped to restore some of Langley's credibility. Much of the criticism he received was directed at the "sheer lunacy" of even trying to fly. Now that it had been done, Langley looked less like a failure and more like a visionary. Nevertheless, Samuel Langley departed Washington a broken and bitter man. When he died a few years later, Wilbur wrote a gracious note to the Smithsonian stating that the scientist had been a positive influence on their work. Wilbur's comments were more than generous, given the fact that Langley's "influence" had consisted of nothing more than instructing an aide to mail the brothers some articles on aeronautics in 1899, when the Wrights first began their research.

The Smithsonian, trying to recover lost prestige and credibility, issued a surprising and controversial statement in its annual report of 1910 claiming that Langley's *Great Aerodrome,* had it been properly launched, would have been the first craft to fly. Wilbur's comments were edited in such a way that made it appear as if he agreed with their contention. As a result, the report concluded, Langley's machine deserved special place in history as the *world's first* heavier-than-air flying machine *capable* of flight. The brothers were infuriated by such an absurd claim, and a thirty-five-year feud ensued.

In 1914, the Smithsonian was approached by an aviator named Glenn Curtiss who requested permission to reassemble and fly Langley's machine. The Smithsonian, feeling a successful test would settle the matter once and for all, not only gave Curtiss the remnants of the *Great Aerodrome,* it included $2,000 for his trouble. Curtiss was anything but an impartial judge. He was involved in a bitter legal battle with the Wright Company, the airplane manufacturing company founded by the Wright brothers, over the infringement of patents. He knew if he could get Langley's machine in the air, he might upset the Wrights' claim to "pioneer status" on their patent. Curtiss succeeded in flying the *Great Aerodrome,* if you can call skimming along two feet off the surface of the water for fifty yards "flying." At least that's the way an exultant Smithsonian saw it when it issued yet another report supporting its claim.

Declaring Curtiss's pitiful test proof that the *Great Aerodrome* was the first heavier-than-air machine *capable* of flight was particularly offensive to Orville, who, with the death of Wilbur in 1912, carried on the fight alone. The machine Curtiss flew bore little resemblance to Langley's original machine. Although the Smithsonian Institution called the plane an "authentic restoration," it was anything but. Using data and technology created by the Wright brothers, Curtiss made no fewer than thirty-five material alterations to the original design, including installing a Curtiss engine. The changes were never mentioned in the reports issued by the Smithsonian. Nor was the fact that Curtiss stood to benefit substantially by supporting the fraud.

In 1928, Orville Wright received a request from the Smithsonian Institution to send the original *Wright Flyer* to Washington for display in the National Museum. When he learned that the plans were to display the *Flyer* side-by-side with the *Great Aerodrome* (one as the first to fly, the other as the first *capable* of flight), he had enough. Executing a stroke of political genius, Orville shipped the original 1903 *Wright Flyer* to London for display at the British National Museum in South Kensington. Criticism from patriotic Americans was immediate and harsh. In his biography, *The Wright Brothers*, Fred Kelly records Orville's response:

> I believe my course in sending our Kitty Hawk machine to a foreign museum is the only way of correcting the history of the flying machine, which by false and misleading statements has been perverted by the Smithsonian Institution. In a foreign museum this machine will be a constant reminder of the reason of its being there, and after the people and petty jealousies of this day are gone, the historians of the future may examine impartially the evidence and make history accord with it.

The Wright Flyer was sent, with the deep regrets of its patriotic creator, to London, where it would be subjected to German efforts to bomb London into oblivion.

Despite public and congressional pressure to resolve the feud, the battle continued until the early 1940s. Then, thanks to the efforts of Wright biographer Fred Kelly and more pressure from Congress, the feud was resolved. The Smithsonian Institution issued a complete apology, acknowledging not only the Wright brothers as the first to fly but also the *Wright Flyer* as the first machine capable of flight. The damage to the Wrights' credibility, however, had been done. Combined with the patent suits and a small but vocal group of Wright-detractors, an element of doubt had been created in the mind of the public as to whether the Wright brothers were, as one newspaper headline expressed it, "fliers or liars."

SO THE question continues. How did two bicycle builders from Dayton manage to outdo the best scientists and brightest engineers of their day? How could two guys working on the problem part-time, with a little less than $1,000 in the bank to finance the effort, do what others with unlimited resources and time could not? In an effort to come to grips with the question, a number of explanations have been offered over the years. Three stand out from the rest and deserve attention.

How They Did It: The Theories

The "why" portion of the question is easier to answer than the "how" portion, but both are to some degree answerable. Several options emerge in the form of "schools of thought." Let's take a quick look at the most common theories, and then I'll offer my own.

The Caught-in-Fortune's-Wind Theory

One school of thought has it that the Wright brothers were a couple of capable guys who had the good fortune to stumble onto the solution of heavier-than-air, powered and controlled flight. A kind of "blind pig gets lucky" scenario. Some believe that's the only way to explain how two high school "dropouts" from America's heartland managed to do what the best engineers and brightest scientists worldwide could not. The idea of "good fortune" as a reason for the Wright brothers' success is blasted away by the brothers' wind tunnel experiments in 1901. In painstaking fashion over a two-month period, Wilbur and Orville took thousands of measurements of gliding angles and resultant pressures. They then plugged the data into complex trigonometric equations to determine the best wing design to maximize lift. Hardly the stuff of chance.

If there was good fortune involved in the Wright brothers' success, it would rest in the fact that they *were* bicycle builders, and they *were* from Dayton. In *Grand Eccentrics*, a book on Dayton at the dawn of the twentieth century, Mark Bernstein makes the case that growing up there may have been an asset. Dayton was the Silicon Valley of the Midwest at the turn of the century, a hotbed of creativity and invention. In 1870, the city was ranked fifth in patents secured per capita. By 1900, it was first. "Daytonians," Tom Crouch writes in *The Bishop's Boys,* "were feeling very proud of themselves."

Dayton's reputation for spawning innovative talent (inventor Charles Kettering would accumulate more significant patents than any American except Thomas Edison) added to the city's self-confidence, fostering a can-do attitude among its citizens. Bernstein recounts the story of a young woman sailing back from Europe who found herself surrounded shipboard by admirers. The cause for such sudden celebrity? Word had been passed around that the young lady was . . . *from Dayton!* "They acted," she reported, "like they were meeting someone from a place where things were happening."

> Dayton was the Silicon Valley of the Midwest at the turn of the century, a hotbed of creativity and invention.

The Wright brothers' choice of occupation must be considered fortunate as well. While the brothers were addressing the challenge of heavier-than-air manned flight, the world was infatuated with power. Giant machines, most steam-driven, captivated people everywhere. Automobile makers were developing bigger and more powerful motors to satisfy the demand of customers. When Hiram Maxim, inventor of the machine gun, took on the problem of manned flight, he focused his efforts on the motors that would power flying machines. His "solution" was a behemoth powered by two engines capable of generating a whopping 360 horsepower between them. Maxim never got his machine off the ground, which was fortunate, since he never bothered to create a means to control it.

As bicycle builders, Wilbur and Orville understood a thing or two about balance and control. Bicycles, by their very nature, are inherently unstable. Nevertheless, that instability can be overcome in a reasonably short time by superior design and operator skill. Because of their work, the Wright brothers knew instinctively that balance and control would be the keys to heavier-than-air flight, and they directed their first efforts there. To say, however, that the Wright brothers were a couple of Midwesterners who fiddled

> If the Wright brothers *were* caught in fortune's wind, they were setting the sails and choosing the direction.

around and got lucky is absurd. If the Wright brothers *were* caught in fortune's wind, they were setting the sails and choosing the direction.

The All-in-the-Family Theory

Another explanation puts forth the proposition that the Wright brothers' accomplishments were the result of some sort of genetic predisposition. There's no doubt that the ability of Wilbur and Orville to think in a clear, disciplined fashion was inherited from their father. It was from Milton Wright, a minister and later bishop in the United Brethren Church, that the brothers would inherit their tenacity and persistence. A strong-willed and self-assured man, Bishop Wright never let anything distract him from a course of action he believed to be correct. At the same time, he was open to other points of view. The result was a hunger for knowledge, a commitment to integrity of thought, and a willingness to consider the ideas of others, all of which would be passed along to Wilbur and Orville.

Legend has it that the Wright brothers inherited their mechanical aptitude from their mother. The Bishop, some say, couldn't drive a nail straight! There's a substantial amount of truth here. Susan Catherine Wright was the daughter of John Gottlieb Koerner, a carriage and cabinetmaker. As a young girl, she enjoyed watching her father work and loved spending time in his workshop. She undoubtedly picked up much of her mechanical aptitude watching her father fashion his creations. Although this was unusual for the time, Koerner may have even allowed his daughter to assist him on a few projects.

With Bishop Wright frequently away on church business, Susan kept the farm and home functioning smoothly. Noted for her cleverness and ingenuity, she repaired household items whenever they were broken. Sometimes, she took common utensils and converted them into clever and useful gadgets. Her family used to say, "Mother can mend anything!" When her older sons, Lorin and Reuchlin, were boys, she helped them design and build their first sled. It became a prized family heirloom. Wilbur and Orville had an opportunity to learn cleverness and ingenuity just by observing their mother at work. But she did more than let them observe. She encouraged their own creative efforts as well.

Although traits inherited from their parents certainly equipped Wilbur and Orville to take on the challenge of heavier-than-air flight, attributing the brothers' success to lineage alone would be an overemphasis of the point. Reuchlin and Lorin, older siblings of Wilbur and Orville, "swam" in the same genetic pool, but neither of them achieved anything of note. Their sister Katharine graduated from Oberlin College at a time when women stayed at home and cared for their families, then did just that. Genetic history merits mention, but only as part of a larger, more complete picture.

The Sheer Genius Theory

This explanation posits that Wilbur and Orville Wright were natural geniuses who simply overwhelmed the problem through the sheer power of their intellect. Alex Roland, a history professor at Duke University, doesn't mince words when describing the brothers. "They were geniuses," he exudes, "just absolute geniuses." Although many would agree with Roland, one who wouldn't was Wilbur. When it was suggested by a friend that their invention was the result of genius, Wilbur responded:

> Do you not insist too strongly on the single point of mental ability? To me, it seems like a thousand other factors, each rather insignificant in itself, in the aggregate influence the event ten times more than mere mental ability or inventiveness.

I'm sure that modesty and graciousness influenced Wilbur's response, but I don't think that was the reason for it. I believe attributing their success to genius alone is superficial and lacks an understanding of, and appreciation for, what they did. I believe Wilbur saw their invention as a product of many things, one of which was an understanding of the problem-solving process and its role in guiding them through the various aspects of the heavier-than-air challenge.

The biggest problem with the "genius myth" is that it leads us away from an important ingredient, important not only in terms of what it provided the Wright brothers, but also in terms of what it can provide us. There is much today's business reader can learn from the Wright brothers. Their lives and work are a treasure trove of ideas, concepts, and principles that can be used today to improve problem-solving skills.

Guided by Principle(s)

For nearly a hundred years, the story of the Wright brothers has been presented as a biographical profile, technical overview, or combination of the two. No one, it seems, has pulled from the story the governing precepts that fueled their drive to success. In *The Wright Way*, I've tried to connect the dots between the achievements of Wilbur and Orville Wright and the problem-solving principles that guided their steps. My goal is not, as Peter Jakab so ably does in *Visions of a Flying Machine,* to take the reader through a step-by-step analysis of the technical aspects of the invention process. My goal is to take a macro look, attempting to make the case that what the Wright brothers achieved was the result of a well-conceived and methodical application of identifiable problem-solving principles.

The Wright brothers not only solved the problem, they left behind extraordinary records detailing the steps they took in the process. From their lives, journals, and research data we gain not only a solution to manned flight, but a keen look into their thinking. In so doing, we see a problem-solving model emerge that can be applied to any business problem, challenge, or opportunity today. My goal is to present the principles, then energize them with bits and pieces of the Wright brothers' journey. The story by itself is extraordinary. The fact that it has practical application to business only adds to its impact.

A Great Collaboration

Wilbur and Orville were remarkably different, but it was what they shared in common that made their partnership work. It was out of these pockets of similarity, I believe, that their problem-solving strategy, and the principles that powered it, emerged. For example, the sons of a United Brethren minister, Wilbur and Orville shared a solid moral foundation rooted in justice and integrity. The bitter fights with Glenn Curtiss (over patent infringement) and the Smithsonian (over false claims) were, more than anything, a result of their inability to accommodate dishonesty in any form. This shared passion for the truth enabled the brothers to engage in heated, often argumentative, discussions on ideas and theories without having to concern themselves about the motives of the other. Both knew each had the same objective—uncover truth—and were able to "let it out" in heated debates. Their fidelity to purpose allowed the brothers to use a problem-solving exercise I call "forging," or the principle of constructive conflict.

Wilbur and Orville benefited jointly from a family culture that emphasized the Protestant work ethic. Included in that was a strong belief that time and money were not to be wasted. These character traits were revealed in the need to work in an orderly and methodical fashion that emphasized efficiency and effectiveness. This required the brothers to plan their work. Time and money were saved by prioritizing responsibilities. We call it project management today, but the gist was the same: Tackle the toughest parts of a problem or project first in order to waste the least amount of time should it be, for any reason, an unachievable goal. This would emerge in the form of a problem-solving technique I call "tackle the tyrant," the principle of worst things first.

Both brothers shared a mutual love for tinkering, although they approached it in different ways. Orville was a tactile tinkerer who liked to get his hands on things. Even as a young boy, he loved taking mechanical things apart to see how they worked. Not only was he adept at putting them back together, but he often did so in improved fashion. Wilbur was comfortable at a workbench as well, but his strength was conceptual tinkering. He liked to turn ideas over in his mind, looking for relatedness and connections, similarities and contrasts. The brothers' passion for tinkering with things and ideas emerges in a problem-solving technique I call "fiddling," the principle of inveterate tinkering.

The Wright brothers, organized and structured in so many ways, shared a remarkable ability to seek out and seriously consider "out of the box" solutions. Their ability to slide effortlessly between the concrete and the abstract allowed them to surface and consider ideas that would otherwise go untapped. This mental process—flexible thought projected against rigid structure—allowed the brothers to consider, then adopt, a critical component of a successful flying machine: wing-warping. This ability of the brothers is presented in a creative thinking and problem-solving process I call "mind-warping," the principle of rigid flexibility.

Both brothers shared a passion for learning that found its most common expression in reading. Wilbur's love of books was powered by his scholarly nature, Orville's by insatiable curiosity. They both, however, arrived at the same destination. Books and an accompanying thirst for knowledge defined their work from start to finish. Even at Kitty Hawk, just days before the historic flights, personal diaries document that spare time was dedicated to reading. Three days before his flight, Orville was "practicing up" on his German and French. This love of books and knowledge emerges in a problem-solving concept I call "relentless preparation," or the principle of forever learning.

One of the more remarkable traits the brothers shared, in light of such different personality styles, was an appreciation (bordering on obsession) for detail. They were precise craftsmen who took extraordinary pride in the quality of their work. That pride was expressed in the exactness of thought that went into their theories and calculations, as well as the accurate workmanship of their hands. This exactness reveals itself in a problem-solving concept I call "measure twice," or the principle of methodical meticulousness.

Wilbur and Orville shared an innate decency that somehow managed to survive the suffocating pressure of gushing praise and lofty acclaim. The brothers became, for a period of time, the two most famous men on the planet. Yet their humility, a modesty that required them to put the needs of others (especially family) before their own, somehow remained intact. Their sense of decency is expressed toward each other in the form of equitable treatment. The biblical urging to "prefer your brother" (i.e., regard him greater than you regard yourself) is reflected in a partnership characterized by its fidelity of purpose and personal devotion. This is expressed in a problem-solving concept I call "force multiplication," the principle of equitable teamwork.

For those who are searching for an answer to the "why these guys" question, the answer may lie in what the brothers held in common that emerged from their work as a viable, if not formalized, problem-solving model. It is a model based on seven principles I call *The Wright Way*. And it is the model that enabled the brothers to exploit one other area of similarity: a passionate belief that man could fly.

CHAPTER THREE

FORGING

THE PRINCIPLE OF CONSTRUCTIVE CONFLICT

*Where there is much desire to learn, there of necessity
will be much arguing.*
John Milton (1608–1674), English poet

FORGING is a problem-solving principle that uses constructive conflict
to uncover and validate new ideas and strategies. Like a blacksmith's forge,
ideas are subjected to the "heat" of discussion and the "blows" of contention until a practical solution begins to take shape.

*   *   *

If you happened to be walking down West Third Street in Dayton,
Ohio, during the summer of 1900, and passed by a bicycle shop with its
doors and windows propped open to catch a cooling breeze, you might
have been startled to hear two high-pitched voices yelling at each other
at the top of their lungs. Your first inclination might have been to find a
policeman to break up the fight! But if you lived in the neighborhood,

you probably paid little attention to it. Locals had grown accustomed to the intense discussions of Wilbur and Orville Wright and probably just thought, "The boys are at it again." To the untrained ear, it was mayhem, a lot of crazy shouting and arguing over this theory or that idea. And it didn't end with the close of business.

It wasn't unusual for an argument, begun in the workshop on the second floor of their bicycle business, to be resumed later in the evening. After dinner, the brothers would head to the front parlor in their home on Hawthorn Street and pick up where they had left off at work. Orville, who preferred a wooden-backed chair, would sit ramrod straight with arms folded akimbo. Wilbur, who preferred slouching in a stuffed chair, would clasp hands behind his head and extend his long legs out into the room. After a moment, Orville would take exception to an idea Wilbur had expressed hours earlier, as if his brother had just spoken the words. Wilbur would reply, "Tis." "Tisn't," said Orville. And the chase was on. Their arguing would sometimes grow so intense that Carrie Kayler, the Wright housekeeper, would peek into the room to make sure the brothers weren't about to come to blows! It may have been alarming to Carrie, but to Wilbur and Orville, it was the sound of discovery.

Learning to Scrap

Orville and Wilbur Wright were devoted to each other. "In some cases," says historian Scott Dennis, "people thought it was like one spirit in two bodies." Although four years separated them, they couldn't have been closer if they'd been identical twins. Wilbur once commented, "From the time we were little children, my brother Orville and myself lived together, worked together, and in fact, thought together." Wilbur did not mean to imply, however, that they had the *same thoughts!* Although alike in many ways, especially in terms of character and values, they were remarkably different in personality traits and thinking styles. J. G. Crowther, in *Six Great Inventors,* writes: "The unique bond of intellectual collaboration was not based on similarity of temperaments, but rather on contrast." These differences, as often as not, would

These differences would emerge in the form of lively discussions Wilbur liked to call "scraps."

emerge during their work in the form of lively discussions Wilbur liked to call "scraps."

By all accounts agreeable and well-mannered young men, Wilbur and Orville were not immune to the rivalries and arguments typical of siblings. Possessing strong wills and independent points of view (traits inherited from their father), they often saw things differently as children. Rather than reel in his sons when squabbles erupted, Milton Wright taught them to argue productively. In the evening, after finishing their meal, the boys would remain at the table. Their father would introduce a topic, which the brothers were "encouraged" to debate. The debates, which often grew contentious, were allowed to continue as long as they were not disrespectful. After a period of time, the father would instruct his sons to change sides. Wilbur was required to defend Orville's position, and vice versa. It was a skill that would serve them well later as bicycle builders and aviation pioneers, because their sometimes thunderous discussions *produced results.*

As they grew older and began to work together on various projects and ventures, Wilbur and Orville learned to make their conflicts purposeful. "In time," writes Tom Crouch in *The Bishop's Boys,* "they would learn to argue in a more efficient way, tossing ideas back and forth in a kind of verbal shorthand until a kernel of truth began to emerge." The brothers learned how to disagree, and at times took delight in doing so. "I love to scrap with Orv," Wilbur once commented, "Orv's a good scrapper." Beyond enjoying the contesting of ideas, Wilbur saw practical benefits. "Discussion brings out new ways of looking at things," he noted, "and helps round off the corners." Constructive conflict was an important part of their collaborative effort, one that influenced every aspect of their work. They became, in effect, a two-man brainstorming team with prolific output.

A Rough-and-Tumble Game

During their experiments at Kill Devil Hills, Wilbur and Orville were sometimes joined by George Spratt, a young medical student from Coatsville, Pennsylvania. Spratt, an aeronautical enthusiast and confidant of Wright mentor Octave Chanute, was working on some flying theories and had written the Wright brothers to run his ideas past them. Wilbur approached the matter in the same fashion he and Orville had found so effective. In *Wilbur and Orville: A Biography of the Wright Brothers,* Fred Howard notes that Wilbur tried to engage Spratt in their "rough and tumble game" of bouncing ideas off each other. Spratt, finding the exercise intimidating, backed away from his initial proposals. Wilbur was not pleased. "I see that you are back to your old trick of giving up before you are half-beaten in an argument," he wrote Spratt. "I felt pretty certain of my own ground," he continued, "but was anticipating the pleasure of a good scrap before the matter was settled."

Forging

When Wilbur and Orville launched into one of their "spirited debates," they were applying a problem-solving principle I call *forging.* If you look the word up in the dictionary, you'll see a variety of definitions, ranging from the hammering of metal to the writing of bad checks. It also means to surge forward with a sudden burst of speed, a need that many companies certainly have. To these definitions, I'd like to add another. Forging is:

> A form of constructive conflict where ideas are subjected to the "heat" of discussion and the "blows" of contention until a practical solution begins to take shape.

The objective of forging is to not only surface new ideas, but to thrust them forward. The forging analogy came to me while visiting the Wright brothers' home and bicycle business in, of all places, Michigan.

A Tribute to Innovation

If you want to see the house in which Orville was born and Wilbur died, or see the Wright Cycle Company where the brothers constructed the original *Wright Flyer,* you'll have to go to Dearborn and visit Greenfield Village, Henry Ford's national museum to American technology and history. Concerned that America might lose touch with the foundations of its greatness, Ford purchased many of the original buildings that had given birth to such miracles as manned flight and the electric light bulb. Thomas Edison's Menlo Park laboratory, the Wright brothers' home and bicycle shop (relocated from Dayton in 1938), Ford's first automobile assembly plant—all are integral parts of this living tribute to ingenuity and innovation.

In addition to being a showcase of famous homes and workplaces, Greenfield Village is a functioning community with artisans demonstrating skills common in America two hundred years ago. My personal favorite is a Cotswold-style blacksmith's shop located on the backside of the park where the forging process can be seen in action. The last time I was there, two men were making strap hinges for use in repairing a garden gate. As I watched the men at work, I realized the process, which at first glance seemed random and chaotic, actually had a cadence and order to it.

While an apprentice pumped a set of bellows, turning nuggets of coal into a cherry-hot fire, the blacksmith selected an ingot from a nearby pile. When the forge had reached the proper temperature, the "smithy" used a set of tongs to insert the metal into the fire until it turned the desired color. The glowing member was then laid on the anvil where smithy and apprentice took turns striking it with heavy hammers, each blow sending a shower of pinpoint sparks cascading into the air. Slowly, the metal began to conform to the intentions of its masters. Out of the fire and sparks of the coal-fired forge emerged the "solution."

Forging, The Wright Way

When Wilbur and Orville subjected their ideas to each other's scrutiny, it was the equivalent of sticking them into the cherry-hot fire of a forge. As the debate heated, they withdrew their ideas from the fire and laid them upon the anvil of reason. As they challenged each other's positions, their unshaped ideas and opinions were hammered into the form of a potential solution. It was a skill that would be applied in some form every step of the way, from the parlor, where the idea of a flying machine was first debated, to the cow pastures of Huffman Prairie, where their flyer was perfected. Their conflicts generated the energy that fueled their creativity.

> As they challenged each other's positions, their unshaped ideas and opinions were hammered into the form of a potential solution.

The Wright brothers used the concept of forging (i.e., constructive conflict) to perfection in uncovering new ideas and approaches to the problems and challenges they tackled. When Wilbur noted that he loved to scrap with Orville, he wasn't referring to some perverted satisfaction gained from fighting. He was talking about the usefulness of the exercise in stimulating creative thinking. When scrapping with his brother, Wilbur knew he was up against a worthy "opponent," and that he would be forced to think his position through carefully. It was a process the brothers used to validate their theories, sorting through the strengths and weaknesses of each. Constructive conflict was a key component of their problem-solving model.

Orv's a Good Scrapper

The first time I read Wilbur's quote ("Orv's a good scrapper"), the first question that came to mind was, "Why?" What was it about Orville that made him a "worthy opponent" for Wilbur, who could be intimidating at times. The answer is worth pursuing as we seek to gain a better understanding of the forging process. Here's my list of traits that I think made Wilbur appreciate Orville's combativeness:

→ *Tough mental honesty.* Wilbur knew that Orville would not resort to "gamesmanship" in arguing, that feeble strategy employed by those who value "winning" more than learning. His fidelity to purpose was one constant Wilbur could count on. The importance of factual accuracy was a key part of Orville's personality; it was not within his makeup to depart from it. At the same time, he had the character and courage not to be cowed by Wilbur if he felt he had the better case. He was more than capable of standing his ground against Wilbur's intense and intimidating rebuttals.

→ *High-spirited enthusiasm.* Although their personality styles were markedly different—Wilbur the visionary, Orville the detail person—Wilbur knew that Orville would give him a spirited effort. No matter how passionately Wilbur defended his position, he knew Orville would not concede until he had made his point. The goal with the brothers was not consensus, but convergence—a blending of ideas that yielded the strongest options.

→ *Focused listening.* In *Wright Reminiscences,* Ivonette Wright Miller recalls her two famous uncles as being adept at "arguing and *listening.*" Wilbur knew he would not have to repeat himself because Orville was not paying attention. Since the purpose of their arguments was to uncover the truth, both men wanted to hear the point of view of the other. Orville knew how to listen for ideas and alternate meanings as well as words.

• *Open (flexible) thinking.* Orville was not given to "falling in love" with his ideas. If it was necessary to revise his initial position, he was able to do so. When the problem under discussion needed to be addressed sequentially, Orville's disciplined mind allowed him to do so. But his ability to process information in parallel fashion (we call it multitasking today) gave him the flexibility to slip easily in and out of "the box."

• *Confident self-image.* Orville was, by nature, a cheerful optimist. In his scraps with Wilbur, he was able to disassociate his self-image from the idea he was defending. Since he did not take his arguments with Wilbur as a personal attack, he was able to fiercely defend his positions without losing his enthusiasm for the process. Orville was also adept at using his humor to defuse a situation if it was getting out of hand. And Wilbur knew he could "let it all out" with Orville without having to worry about an argument escalating into anger.

Although a few of these traits were unique to Orville in their relationship, most could be applied to Wilbur as well, which is why the process worked. The one thing that sustained their ability to contest each other so passionately, which was critical to the whole process, was the unfailing *trust* and *respect* they had for each other. Both found their quarrels, as author Logan Smith said, "great emancipations."

From the Wrights' perspective, the benefits of scrapping were worthwhile. In addition to "rounding off the corners," Wilbur and Orville discovered that their debating often served to clear the air of "stagnant thinking." By forcing each other to defend their position, they were able to discard ideas with little merit. In addition to clearing away the dross, the process served to reveal new ideas and approaches that became the stuff of future inventions and discoveries. Their scrapping was a creative life force

Their scrapping was a creative life force that energized the brothers, driving them forward in their quest to fly.

that energized the brothers, driving them forward in their quest to fly. Not only that, it was an exercise the brothers enjoyed.

Scrapping for Orville and Wilbur Wright was a way to test their ideas, to put them in the fires of their "mental forge." Never was the Wright brothers' use of forging more in evidence than in the final months leading up to Orville's historic flight in December 1903. The brothers had been moving methodically toward completing their flyer when a problem cropped up from an unexpected quarter, a problem that caught them both off guard by its surprising complexity.

Fire Up the Forge!

When Wilbur and Orville were prioritizing the various subsets of the flying problem, the propeller was placed low on the list. Neither had thought it would pose a problem, since propellers of the marine screw variety had been around for over a century. They thought it would be quick work to access data needed on efficiency, thrust, and other elements, then adapt it to their need. What they discovered, however, was that no such information existed. For over a hundred years, companies manufacturing marine screws (propellers) had done so without equations or formulas to guide them. A part of their flying machine the Wright brothers expected to pose little problem would become one of their most challenging.

The Wright brothers had to start from scratch on the propeller problem, and they did so under considerable pressure. The men knew that Samuel Langley, their chief competitor in the race to fly, was close to making an attempt. The propeller problem not only needed to be solved, it needed to be solved fast. In June 1903, Orville wrote George Spratt, "During the time the engine was building we were engaged in some very heated discussions on the principles of screw propellers." What the brothers soon realized was that the problem would tax them to the hilt—physically and mentally.

Orville would later note that it was hard to even find a place to start. As they considered the problem, they realized there was no easy way into it. "What at first seemed a simple problem," Orv later recalled, "became more complex the more we studied it." The machine was moving forward, the air was flying backward, and the propellers were turning sideways. Nothing, it seemed, was standing still. The biggest challenge they faced was figuring where to begin. As usual, the starting spot for the brothers was a spirited debate of the possibilities.

Charlie Taylor, the Wright Cycle Company's only employee and chief mechanic, said that the air in the room above him where the brothers worked was "frightened with argument." Both brothers had high voices that rose even higher in argument, and at times, Taylor couldn't tell who was arguing which point. Taylor later recounted:

> Both the boys had tempers, but no matter how angry they ever got, I never heard them use a profane word. The boys were working out a lot of theory in those days, and occasionally they would get into terrific arguments. They'd shout at each other something terrible. I don't think they really got mad, but they sure got awfully hot.

Taylor later recalled one fierce argument the propeller problem had occasioned. The morning after their scrap, Orville came into the shop and told Wilbur he felt like he might have been wrong in his point of view. Wilbur, who had continued to evaluate Orville's arguments overnight, said he was inclined to agree with Orville's approach. Taylor said, "The first thing I knew they were arguing the thing all over again, only this time they had switched ideas." It was the very strategy their father had taught them as young boys debating at the dinner table.

The constructive conflict Wilbur and Orville engaged in, a process that often made others uncomfortable, was in fact essential to their inventive method. "Their ability to defend their point of view with real passion," Tom Crouch notes in *The Bishop's Boys,* "while at the same time listening to the other fellow's opinion, was an essential part of the process." As they argued through the problem step-by-step, the brothers were "rounding off the corners," and when they were through, they knew what had to be done. More important, they knew how.

Going Along to Get Along

Constructive conflict as a creative option has fallen on hard times at companies that perceive it as a negative exercise. In the interest of political correctness and civility, we've shifted the emphasis from the pursuit of creativity to the preservation of pleasantness. Some of this is the residue of our fascination in the late 1980s and early 1990s with Japanese management techniques, which emphasized the importance of reaching con-

In the interest of political correctness and civility, we've shifted the emphasis from the pursuit of creativity to the preservation of pleasantness.

sensus. The goal was to leave no one dissatisfied or frustrated, to seek unity and solidarity on every issue. The problem, as English philosopher Alfred North Whitehead noted, is that "periods of tranquility are seldom prolific of creative achievement." Japanese management has been discarded by many of its early proponents who now see the value in occasionally stirring things up.

Companies that agree not to disagree rob themselves of an effective problem-solving tool capable of generating significant, positive results. Instead of viewing conflict as the furnace in which new ideas are forged, many fear it as a destructive force that might lead to a corporate meltdown. "People's tendency to avoid conflict, to duck tough issues," writes Chris Argyris in the *Harvard Business Review,* "becomes institutionalized and leads to a culture that can't tolerate straight talk." I believe many companies avoid (even dread) conflict because participants:

- Do not trust the motives of the other members

- Are not prepared to intelligently defend their positions

- Do not want to risk possible "loss of face"

- Equate conflict with "winning" and "losing"

- Do not want to put the status quo "at risk"

- Are afraid that "losing" will lead to unwanted changes

- Don't feel "safe" in expressing their opinions

It's surprising that so many people have negative feelings toward constructive conflict. Especially when you consider that few issues in business, most of which involve fighting over limited resources, are ever resolved without a battle of some sort.

Nonverbal Feedback

A colleague of mine works for a company that holds a monthly management meeting chaired by its president. Although they have a talented group of people with strongly held ideas on how to do things, he characterizes the meetings as docile and lackluster. It seems that everyone who joins the company quickly learns about the president's style of "nonverbal" communication. It used to be that if the president didn't like your point of view, he'd just explode. Realizing this was stifling the flow of ideas, he decided to become a "nonparticipant" in the meetings by not speaking. Without uttering a word, however, he still managed to communicate his thoughts. Whenever he took exception to what was said, a vein on his forehead would begin to swell. Instead of a spirited discussion where ideas were tested in the forge of reason, the focus of the entire meeting was on one tiny, but steadily growing, blood vessel!

A quick search on the Internet reveals an abundance of consultants specializing in conflict management and mediation (there is no shortage of companies engaging in *destructive* conflict). It's interesting to note, however, that most of those specializing in conflict management do not propose eliminating conflict completely. Jagoda Perich-Anderson, an organizational consultant and conflict mediator, says some companies need to increase—not reduce—the amount of conflict in their organizations. "We need to learn to become more comfortable and skillful with conflict," she says. Perich-Anderson suggests there are three keys to making conflict a plus: mutual respect, a spirit of curiosity, and a commitment to learning. Once you have completed this book, you will see that all three qualities were abundantly present in Wilbur and Orville Wright.

The key to selling and implementing this creative process is to reverse the negative mind-set by making a clear distinction between "constructive" conflict and "competitive" conflict. Arguing does not mean you are working at cross-purposes. Several years ago I worked for a small company that manufactured electronic components. The president of the company, an easygoing fellow who valued and encouraged teamwork, would often (and surprisingly) get in fiery arguments with our engineers. In product planning sessions, he could be as hardheaded and opinionated as anyone. To the casual observer hearing the raised voices in the conference room, a pitched battle would seem to be under way.

These sessions were the strength of our company. Instead of the "stretch sock" (i.e., "one size fits all") mentality of our competitors, we gained a strong reputation in the market for our ability to create cost-effective, nonstandard options for our customers. Our ideas were noted for their innovation, as well as their application to the customer's specific need. In addition, we took great pride in presenting our customers with multiple options, rather than the take-it-or-leave-it approach of our competitors. It was easy for us to do this, since constructive conflict frequently generated multiple possibilities. Our competitive edge—solutions to specific needs—was a by-product of constructive conflict. Even presidents use this strategy.

I was listening to an interview on Fox News with an adviser to President Bush, who was asked to describe the president's style in his staff meetings. The aide indicated that the president did not discourage contention in his meetings, feeling that a spirited debate would bring forth new ideas, while serving to validate or eliminate others. The aide went on to explain that National Security Advisor Condoleezza Rice, who is responsible for meeting management, is encouraged by the president to let the process "play itself out." Dr. Rice, the aide noted, does not try to "soften the edges." As long as trust and respect are maintained, there is no need to restrict what is, under the right circumstances, an effective tool in creative problem solving. "A little rebellion now and then," said Thomas Jefferson, "is a good thing." That makes two presidents that agree with me.

Products (Benefits) of the Forge

The Wright brothers used the forging process to perfection. Many of the theories they "hammered" into solutions remain in use a hundred years later. Not many inventors can boast that kind of staying power. Wilbur and Orville found the process enormously effective, and so will you. Some of the practical benefits of forging include:

➤ It helps to bring new ideas and approaches to the surface.

➤ It forces individuals to think through their ideas intelligently.

➻ It exposes "cracks" (e.g., mistakes, potential weakness) in ideas.

➻ It challenges participants to be more original in their thinking.

➻ It increases teamwork, awareness, and concept "buy-in."

➻ It helps "clear the air" (i.e., relieve tension).

Forging is an excellent tool for affecting change. An increase in the level of discontent with the status quo can be a great tool for generating new ideas.

Before Stoking the Furnace

Although the benefits of constructive conflict are many, there are a few things to consider before introducing it in your organization. Implementation should begin with an honest assessment of the company's culture and emotional climate. Does senior leadership encourage participation or "hammer down" differing points of view? Does the company have a culture of trust and teamwork, or does mistrust and cynicism prevail? Among the things to consider before "forging" ahead are:

➻ Levels of competitiveness (especially interdepartmental)

➻ Corporate and individual risk-taking propensity

➻ Levels of trust, cooperation, and openness

➻ Individual egos and personalities

➻ Tendency toward groupthink (i.e., conformity of thought)

➻ Current levels of employee participation

➻ Past history in resolving conflicts

➻ Existing levels of friction and tension

My wife, who brainstormed with me on the principles in this book, liked the concept of forging, but she was concerned by the potential risks that may be involved. Interestingly, she thought it would work in her own company because of the strong sense of shared purpose felt by employees.

"It would work for us," she said, "because we all want the same thing: our clients satisfied." Her concern, however, is a valid one, which is why the points in the aforementioned list should be carefully considered.

Well-Digging

In August 1902, the Wright brothers headed to Kill Devil Hills with the best glider they had ever built. Using the data they had gleaned from their wind tunnel experiments the winter before, they now knew exactly what wing design would provide the best lift and the least drag. There was one nagging problem, however, and it occurred again on September 23. Orville was attempting a turn when one wing went high while the other went low. The glider spun wildly out of control, crashing into the sand from a height of thirty feet. The result, as Orville recounts in his diary entry that night, "was a heap of flying machine, cloth, and sticks . . . with me in the center without a bruise or a scratch."

The problem Wilbur and Orville were encountering about one out of every fifty glides was a potentially fatal one. The action the brothers were encountering, which they called "well-digging," would later be known as a tailspin. As long as the brothers made straight glides or gentle turns, the glider performed as designed. If they attempted tighter turns, or encountered a reduction in speed, the machine would become unmanageable, spinning out of control until it hit the ground with heart-stopping impact. Regardless of its name, it was a terrifying experience that happened to both Wilbur and Orville.

After Orville's crash, the brothers suspended glides, choosing to fly their glider as a kite in an effort to understand what was happening. Toward the end of September 1902, they were joined by their brother Lorin and, a day later, George Spratt. On the evening of October 2, the three brothers and Spratt sat together discussing the well-digging problem. As usual with Wilbur and Orville, the conversation grew contentious, a situation that always made Spratt uncomfortable. Watching Orville waving his arms about as he made a point, or hearing Wilbur respond in staccato, machine-gun fashion, was not a process Spratt enjoyed.

During their probing arguments that evening, Orville consumed more coffee than usual. Whether it was the extra caffeine or the adrenaline rush from their late-night "rough and tumble" debate, Orville couldn't sleep. As he lay awake in his bed, he began mentally walking through the problems they were encountering. Not only was Orville a good scrapper, he was an excellent listener. Now, as he reviewed Wilbur's ideas and blended them with his own, the solution to the problem came to him. The next morning at the breakfast table, he laid out the problem in orderly fashion, then presented his solution.

Orville's idea, refined by additional suggestions from Wilbur (i.e., invention-extension), would not only give the Wright brothers a controllable glider, it would provide the last link in what would become a patentable process. The Wright brothers' debate had once more produced results. In *How We Invented the Airplane,* Orville wrote, "In the seven or eight hundred gliding flights we made after the adjustable rudder was installed, not once did we encounter the difficulty we had experienced." By continually challenging each other, probing each other's arguments for flaws or weaknesses, Wilbur and Orville were able to unscramble difficult problems and issues. Practicing unfailing mental honesty at all times, the objective was never to win, but to uncover the truth.

A Troubling Process

When Wilbur and Orville tried to engage George Spratt in debate, Spratt pushed back. In a letter sent to Wilbur after he returned to Pennsylvania, Spratt complained that the process was troubling to him. He was particularly put off by the brothers' habit of switching sides in the middle of an argument, a strategy he described as "dishonest." Wilbur replied in a letter to Spratt:

> It was not my intention to advocate dishonesty in argument nor a bad spirit in a controversy. No truth is without some mixture of error, and no error so false but that it possesses no element of truth. If a man is in too big a hurry to give up an error, he is liable to give up some truth with it, and in accepting the arguments of the other man he is sure to get some errors with it. Honest argument is merely a process of mutually picking the beams and motes out of each other's eyes so both can see clearly. Men become wise just as they become rich, more by what they save than by what they

receive. After I get hold of a truth I hate to lose it again, and I like to sift all the truth out before I give up on an error.

Wilbur's response is worth keeping in mind as you sell your organization on the process. Although it may take time for forging to evolve into an efficient and productive tool in your company, don't bail out on the process prematurely. It took a few years for Wilbur and Orville's "scrapping" to become an effective problem-solving tool in their work.

Learning to Soar

Bear in mind that forging may not work for everyone. It is, however, a highly productive technique that need not be feared. Care, however, must be taken to do it right. Here are several suggestions for making constructive conflict an effective part of your company's problem-solving culture:

- *Assess first.* Begin with an honest appraisal of the organization's emotional climate, making sure it's conducive to forging. If the company's culture will not support contesting each other's ideas without creating emotional scars, there may be more pressing issues to address first.

- *Establish the objective.* When the Wright brothers contested each other's ideas, their objective was not to win a point, but to get at the truth. In their discussions, the goal was always to get at the correct answers, no matter who possessed them. Make sure participants understand this objective in the forging process.

- *Keep it lively but civil.* Wilbur and Orville perfected the art of arguing without getting angry. A loss of civility was never a part of their process. Make sure everyone participating in constructive conflict understands the difference between arguing and fighting. Encourage everyone to defend their positions with emotion, but not emotionally. Establishing boundaries, or rules for critique, beforehand will create confidence in the process.

- *Periodically take the temperature.* Monitor the process carefully, making sure constructive conflict does not become destructive conflict. If the conflict remains nonemotional, it's most likely safe to proceed. Take care, however, to avoid creating an environment that's too passive to generate results. Be sure to allow transition time at the end for people to "settle down."

➥ *Protect self-images.* Under no circumstances should an individual's self-esteem be injured in the process. One company put up a sign in its conference room that said, "Your ideas will come under attack, but not you." It's the difference between saying, "That's the stupidest idea I ever heard" and "I couldn't disagree with your idea more."

➥ *Don't force it.* Fear will be an inhibitor for some people, so don't force them into the process before they are ready. Those who like constructive conflict will participate; those who don't, will not. Allow those who do not want to engage in the process time to observe. Once they see the process is "safe," they will be more inclined to get involved.

➥ *Periodically switch positions.* The Wright brothers found it useful to change sides in their debates. In the process, each gained a greater understanding of the other's perspective on a problem or issue. Encourage participants in the forging process to periodically defend a position opposed to their own. This will encourage an appreciation for other views, and it will also help to keep the process positive. When switching sides, be sure to allow participants time to reorder their thoughts before resuming the debate.

➥ *Avoid compromise.* Remember that the goal in these sessions is to discover new ideas and approaches, not to reach consensus or compromise. Compromise not only stops the process, it reduces ownership and accountability. Encourage participants to stick to their guns as long as they feel strongly about their position. Make compromise the last resort.

➥ *Include the "uninformed."* Bringing individuals into the problem-solving process who have little or no knowledge of the subjects under consideration can help generate ideas unfettered by prior experience or prejudice. It is not necessary that everyone understand all things in order to argue them effectively, as long as participants are able to look for connections—similarities, contrasts, and parallels—and are encouraged to do so.

•→ *Know when to use it, know when to lose it.* It's important to develop a feel for when forging will work in your company or organization. This process, while useful in a great number of circumstances, is not useful in all of them. When in doubt, discuss it with those who will be asked to participate to get their read on the situation. Encourage team members to initiate the process when they feel it might be effective, and to provide honest feedback when they feel it isn't.

•→ *Know how to exit well.* Encourage participants to aggressively defend points of view, but to bail out on a bad position when necessary. Stay with an opinion only as long as it appears to have merit or serves to stimulate additional discussion. To put it another way, "If the horse is dead, quit riding it." It is the difference between declaring "I quit!" versus saying, "You've answered all my concerns and I'm ready to agree with you."

Remember to keep track of information as it surfaces. You may wish to assign someone to be the recorder, or you may want to "mind map" comments on a whiteboard as they emerge. This step is extremely important, since the final solution may emerge early in the process, not at the end. As the Chinese proverb warns, "A good memory is not as good as a ragged pen."

American educator and philosopher John Dewey, a strong proponent of constructive conflict, saw it as a way to shock nonthinkers out of their "sheep like" passivity. Dewey saw conflict as the "gadfly of thought," a way to energize ingenuity and jump-start the inventive process. It's interesting to note that *gadget* follows *gadfly* in the dictionary. In other words, some new discoveries might just follow a bit of constructive conflict in your company or organization.

One Last Thought

Grover Loening thought he had blown it. After earning a master's degree in aeronautics at Columbia University in 1913, he applied for a position with the Wright Company as an assistant. During his interview with Orville Wright, the discussion veered away from employment to aeronautical design. Loening, speaking in 1971 at a celebration honoring the one-hundredth anniversary of Orville's birth date, recalled that a disagreement had arisen over a point on which Orville was quite positive. Describing himself as "fresh" and "rashly stubborn," Loening disagreed with Orville's position. "In a few moments time I realized that I had become disrespectful and feared I had lost the chance for a new job," Loening recalled. In reality, Orville was quite pleased, even going so far as to goad Loening on. By the end of the interview, Loening had a job offer from the Wright Company. He speculated that he might have gotten the job because Orville missed "scrapping" with Wilbur, who had died the previous year.

In accepting Orville's offer to become his personal assistant, Loening thought he had better be prepared for many such heated discussions with his boss. That was exactly what transpired. He shared the following in his anniversary comments included in Ivonette Wright Miller's book, *Wright Reminiscences:*

> I served as a backdrop for technical analyzing in an inexhaustible manner. Many a night I had to do extra thinking and studying to be prepared to meet Orville's clear, pungent, and devastatingly correct points the next day. What would make this even more exigent, he would remember every word I'd used the day before.

Wilbur and Orville learned how to disagree and took great delight in contesting each other's point of view. The best companies, rather than avoiding conflict, embrace it. They see it as a vital energy source that fuels everything from new product ideas to the marketing strategies that sell them. As Jagoda Perich-Anderson says, "There is argument, but it feels alive and exciting, like something important is happening, like something new might be born." Like the world's first flying machine.

CHAPTER FOUR

TACKLE THE TYRANT

THE PRINCIPLE OF WORST THINGS FIRST

The balancing of a flyer may seem, at first thought, to be a simple matter, yet almost every experimenter had found in this the one point which he could not satisfactorily master.

Wilbur Wright (1867–1912), inventor

TACKLE THE TYRANT is a problem-solving principle based on the idea that within each problem there is a potential "tyrant," a subset of the problem that, if not resolved, will prevent solution of the whole. By putting the worst (i.e., the tyrant problem) first, costs for the whole are limited to this subset should a solution be unachievable.

* * *

You might remember a children's story called "The Three Billy Goats Gruff." A parable, it tells the story of three goats that wanted to cross a river in order to get to the lush, green grass on the opposite side. There was only one way to get across the rushing river, however, and that was to cross a wooden-plank bridge. Under the bridge lurked a troll, an ugly, one-eyed tyrant whose sole mission in life was to eat anyone or anything that tried to cross his bridge. Once, when my mother was reading the story to my daughter, I heard my daughter ask why the goats didn't look for another way to cross the river. "They probably did," Mom replied, "but sooner or later they had to face the tyrant." Therein lies the tale.

A Timely Invitation

In the annals of history, there are items that seem small at their point of occurrence but later emerge as seminal moments. One of these occurred in the history of aviation in the fall of 1901 when Octave Chanute extended an invitation to Wilbur Wright to address the Western Society of Engineers in Chicago. The Wright brothers' relationship with Chanute began in May 1900 when Wilbur, after reading Chanute's book, *Progress in Flying Machines,* had written the Chicago engineer to ask for guidance. It was the beginning of a relationship that would span a decade. The more than four hundred letters exchanged with Chanute between 1900 and 1910 would provide an extraordinary record of how the Wright brothers solved the problem of heavier-than-air flight. In the beginning, Chanute was not just an important source of information, he was a valued sounding board as well, someone the brothers could bounce ideas off in an effort to clarify their thoughts and theories.

Chanute's greatest value to the Wright brothers, however, may have been his role as an encourager. Sensing that Wilbur's enthusiasm was flagging (the brothers had just returned from Kill Devil Hills after a discouraging season of trials), Chanute sought to rouse his protégé from his malaise by inviting him to address this prestigious group of scientists and engineers. Chanute's plan not only served to jump-start Wilbur's interest, it forced him to revisit the research and experiments he and his brother had conducted to date. By performing a step-by-step review of their work, the brothers were able to organize their thinking and get back on track. By the time the review was completed, the brothers knew where they stood, what they believed the critical issues were, and where they would apply their efforts next. It was a breakthrough of the first order for the Wright brothers.

Although technically prepared for his presentation, Wilbur was a little apprehensive about actually giving it. When his sister Katharine asked him whether his speech would be serious or humorous, he replied, "Pathetic." A letter from Chanute a week later didn't help. Chanute wanted to know if Wilbur had any concerns about making the meeting a "ladies night." Wilbur responded that it did not matter to him. "I will already be as badly scared," he wrote, "as it is possible for a man to be." Wilbur's biggest concern was that "ladies night" meant having to come in "full dress" (i.e., formal evening wear). Chanute assured him that would not be necessary.

Clothing was never as important to Wilbur as it was to Orville. Wilbur was no slob, but a crisp trouser crease was a low priority. If Katharine pointed out that his trouser knees were a little baggy, he'd just slip his trousers off and give them a once-over with a heated iron. Orville, on the other hand, was a careful dresser who took pride in his appearance. His clothes were always immaculate. Carrie Kayler, the Wright housekeeper, used to marvel at the fact that Orville could work all day at the machines in the bicycle shop and never get as much as a speck on his clothing. When Wilbur boarded the train for Chicago, he departed wearing Orville's shirt, collar, cuffs, cufflinks, and topcoat. Katharine later wrote her father that Wilbur looked quite good. "Clothes," she wrote, "do make the man."

A Chicago Surprise

On September 18, 1901, Octave Chanute introduced Wilbur Wright to a packed house in Chicago. During his introductory comments, the respected engineer and aviation authority took the opportunity to express some of his thoughts on the flying problem. Chanute made a number of general observations before stating, with surprising conviction, that the lack of a "suitable aeronautical power plant" (i.e., motor) was the greatest obstacle to solving the flying problem. Unless this was addressed and resolved, Chanute continued, heavier-than-air flight was all but impossible. He then introduced, as the night's featured speaker, a man who *couldn't have disagreed* with him more on the views he'd just expressed.

> Wilbur's personal regard for Chanute was trumped by his inability to present anything but what he believed to be true.

Wilbur was taken aback. In earlier correspondence, he had made it clear to Chanute that he and Orville did not believe that power and propulsion were the principal obstacles to manned flight. In fact, at that time the brothers didn't see them as obstacles at all. Wilbur's personal regard for Chanute was trumped by his inability to present anything but what he believed to be true. He had no alternative but to contradict his friend in a highly visible forum. "Compared to the problems of balance and control," Wilbur told those gathered, "all other difficulties are of minor importance." Wilbur further contradicted Chanute's comments by saying, "When this one feature is worked out, the flying age will have arrived." It was not the first time the opposing points of view—power and propulsion versus control and balance—would be contested, especially if Hiram Maxim, Clément Ader, and Samuel Langley were involved.

The Power Team

In the Old Testament of the Bible, God instructs Job (40:15) to "behold now behemoth." Exactly what God was referring to is not known, but we know it must have been something extremely large. Something like an elephant, a giraffe, or Hiram Maxim's flying machine. Hiram Stevens Maxim (1840–1916), an expatriate American living in England, dedicated a considerable portion of his fortune (acquired from his invention of the Maxim machine gun) to the problem of heavier-than-air flight. In fact, he spent in excess of $200,000 constructing a 7,000-pound test rig that would be described in nearly every book on aviation history as a "behemoth." Maxim's machine was powered by two enormous steam engines, each capable of generating 180 horsepower units. The engines, in turn, powered two pusher-style propellers measuring seventeen and a half feet in length. Compared to other craft of the day, this was one huge flying machine.

Maxim's obsession with power was understandable, if not practical. By the end of the nineteenth century, the world's love affair with the motor was in full bloom. Enormous engines had revolutionized life at every level, but their impact was particularly felt in the area of transportation. Like many flying-machine pioneers, Maxim believed that power and propulsion were the key to solving the problem of heavier-than-air flight. In 1892, Maxim boldly announced, "Without doubt the motor is the chief thing to be considered." These practitioners reasoned anything could be made to fly with enough power. To a degree, Maxim proved his point.

In 1894, Maxim and three other men boarded his machine, which was mounted on a test track. On Maxim's signal, the massive structure, powered by 10,000 pounds of brute force, thundered down its one-third-mile track. The machine rose in the air a foot or two before unceremoniously thudding back down to earth. Although technically failing to meet the criteria for a successful flight, Maxim had managed to get his flying machine, remarkable for its lack of aerodynamic qualities, off the ground for a few seconds. It was a powered, though certainly not controlled, flight. Maxim wasn't alone in touting power and propulsion as the answer to achieving flight. In France, Clément Ader was taking a similar, yet somewhat different, approach.

The *Éole*

Ader, a French inventor and telephone pioneer, began work on the heavier-than-air problem in 1872. A self-taught engineer, he studied the problem for years before building a full-size machine he called the *Éole*. Like Maxim, Ader regarded the air as a kind of "stable fluid" through which he could navigate, much like a fish through water. He shared Maxim's view that the answer to the problem lay in generating sufficient propulsion. Instead of building bigger engines, however, Ader's approach was to reduce the craft's weight. Compared to Maxim's 180-horsepower engines, Ader's twenty-horsepower motors were puny. His flying machine, however, was dramatically smaller and lighter than Maxim's. He had more than enough power for the weight. His deficiencies were in other areas.

On October 9, 1890, in a suburb just outside Paris, Clément Ader is said to have made a steam-powered, low-level flight of 160 feet in the *Éole*. The alleged flight remains one of the great mysteries of aviation. If Ader did indeed make the flight, he would have a right to claim the first powered flight in history, a claim that would precede that of the Wright brothers. Only two witnesses saw Ader's flight, however, and they reported that it ended poorly. The *Éole* was said to have crashed at the end due to "deficient equilibrium." Ader's machine had no tail and no practical method of lateral control.

Although a few loyalists still cling to the idea that Ader, not Wilbur and Orville Wright, should be recognized with "first flight" honors, there is little evidence to support the claim. Although Ader was a capable engineer and contributed much to the "flying problem," his legitimacy was called into question when he later claimed to have made a 900-foot flight in his third flying machine, the *Avion III*. Witnesses to this flight state that Ader covered 900 feet, but did so in several hops, with all three wheels never being off the ground at the same time.

Making a Splash

Professor Samuel Langley of the Smithsonian Institution had been working on the flying problem since 1878. Well into his sixties before seriously considering the challenge, Langley also believed the answer to the problem was to develop sufficient power to get the craft in the air. Like Ader, Langley concentrated on reducing the weight of the craft so that a larger engine would not be necessary. Both Langley and Ader, in an effort to maximize power and thrust, committed a grave mistake: They sacrificed structural integrity. Langley's flying machine, named the *Great Aerodrome,* collapsed on takeoff; its light structure was unable to withstand the pressures of launch.

In the larger scheme of things, it was fortunate that Maxim, Ader, and Langley failed to get their machines in the air. Had any of them succeeded, they would have confronted an even greater shortcoming in their machines: the inability to adequately control them. Although Langley had succeeded in flying smaller models of his *Great Aerodrome,* there was no provision for making a turn, and descent was risky at best. What rudders their flying machines did feature were based on a simplistic design so that if they were turned left or right, up or down, the craft would follow in those directions. All three men were of the opinion that control and balance could be worked out later, after mastering straight-line flights. Collectively, Maxim, Ader, and Langley invested nearly half a million dollars (does not include one hundred years of inflation) on their failed machines. Wilbur and Orville Wright took a different approach.

Control and Balance (The Tyrant)

Wilbur and Orville were not just builders of bicycles, they were students of the art. They observed how bicycles handled, and they sought ways to make them more dependable. One discipline of thought overlaid everything they did: study, understand, improve. The brothers' ingenuity was in full force at this time, and improvements to their bicycles were commonplace. They were the first to use balloon tires on their bicycles, greatly improving the comfort of the ride. They made improvements to the coaster brake and invented an oil-retaining hub. New tools began to find their way into the shop of the Wright Cycle Company: a turret lathe, drill press, tube-cutting equipment. They attached the tools to an overhead shaft with pulleys, then designed and built a small illuminating gas-powered engine to drive them. Their bicycles were known for their craftsmanship and attention to detail. More important, the business was making a profit, generating funds that would later be put to good use.

The Wright brothers knew that the key to riding a bicycle was to master its inherent instability. Most of us can remember those terrifying days when we first learned to ride. Some of us were fortunate to have training wheels, but most of us were taught the old-fashioned way. Our parents ran behind us until we worked up a head of steam, then, with one departing shove, left us to our own devices. The inevitable pileups occurred. It wasn't long, however, before we were cruising along shouting, "Look, Mom, no hands!" Without giving it much thought, we overcame the bicycle's greatest shortcoming—its instability. The key element in riding a bicycle was control and balance, and the Wright brothers were well aware of it.

> One discipline of thought overlaid everything they did: study, understand, improve.

A New Hobby

When the Wright brothers first began their flying-machine experiments, it was not with the intent to solve the problem of heavier-than-air manned flight. Fascinated with the exploits of the German glider expert Otto Lilienthal, Wilbur and Orville thought that gliding would be good sport. As the brothers prepared to make their first trip to Kitty Hawk in September 1900, Wilbur wrote his father a letter detailing his plans:

> It is my belief that flight is possible, and while I am taking up the investigation for pleasure rather than profit, I think there is a slight possibility of achieving fame and fortune from it. I am certain I can reach a point much in advance of any previous workers in this field

even if success is not attained just at present. At any rate I will have an outing of several weeks and see a part of the world I have never before visited.

Their first season of gliding was challenging but satisfying to the brothers. As Wilbur later reported, "We considered it quite a point to be able to return without having our pet theories completely knocked in the head by the hard logic of experience, and our own brains dashed out in the bargain."

Pet Theories

Although there were many people addressing the heavier-than-air flying problem, the majority of them were doing it carelessly. They were either assuming too much about the way a flying machine would behave, or leaning too heavily on past experience, causing them to misjudge situations. No one was approaching the problem in the same fashion as Wilbur and Orville Wright. Four years would pass between the date of the brothers' first active interest and their first glide at Kitty Hawk. Those four years would be spent reading, discussing, theorizing, and learning about flight issues. The Wright brothers were looking for what I like to call the "tyrant," that portion of a problem considered most critical and hardest to solve. Before they ever cut a piece of wood or sewed a patch of cloth, the brothers, by thinking the problem through, had identified the worst part of the problem and committed themselves to tackling it first.

Pay as You Go

When Wilbur and Orville began addressing the flying problem in earnest, their intent was to finance the project out of profits generated from their bicycle business. Although they had a bit of money in the bank from an inheritance, the funds available for their experiments were to come from the sale and repair of bicycles. Remarkably, that's exactly what occurred. The brothers never touched the money they had invested. A modest bicycle shop at 1127 West Third Street in Dayton, Ohio (the building now preserved at Greenfield Village), financed the beginning of a billion-dollar industry. With the need to be careful with their money ever in mind, Wilbur and Orville started where they usually did when taking on a new problem—they searched for the "tyrant."

Both Wilbur and Orville were clear, logical thinkers who believed that the starting point in solving any problem was to accurately define the objective. The brothers knew, both intuitively and experientially, that a poorly defined problem can lead one far from the desired outcome. Others had defined the goal simply: "to fly." The Wright brothers expanded the problem definition to include two essential (in their minds) ingredients. Wilbur and Orville wanted to fly *balanced* and *under control*. Instead of concentrating on simply getting off the ground, they gave initial consideration to these more complex issues.

Small Sealed Doors

Wilbur and Orville knew that the flying problem was not simply one big problem, but a number of discrete problems that needed to be addressed individually. It was not, as Wright biographer Fred Howard describes, "one great gate that would fly open when unlocked with a secret key, but rather a series of small sealed doors that would have to be pried open one after another." As the brothers broke down the problem, they discovered that many of the doors had other doors as well. Achieving heavier-than-air powered flight was filled with complexity. Initially, the Wright brothers identified six "doors" (or categories or subsets) within the overall problem. They were:

- Wing design (generating sufficient lift)
- Propulsion (propellers to provide thrust)
- Power (a lightweight, gas-powered engine)
- Control (a means to manage instability in flight)
- Balance (the ability to keep the craft level in flight)
- Flying skill (the ability to actually fly the machine)

The Worst First

As the Wright brothers looked at these various components of the problem, they asked themselves which categories represented the greatest impediment to success. After much study and discussion, the two men agreed that balance and control would be the hardest part of the problem to solve. Having identified balance and control as the "tyrant," the one area capable of blocking their success, they immediately focused their attention there. Since they were funding their research and development out of their own pockets, the Wright brothers had no intention of addressing other issues before this one. They believed that the motor needed to power their craft was already available. The propellers needed to push their craft were also available, or could be made. At the time, sufficient data already existed on wing design, so that would not be an issue, either. Once control and balance were achieved, learning to fly the craft would be possible. They put the worst thing first in an effort to limit their exposure. If they were unable to resolve this issue, they reasoned, their loss would be limited to what was expended on this part of the problem alone.

Many people approach problem solving tentatively. They look for parts of the problem that are familiar to them, that they feel they can comfortably address, then start there in an effort to get things going. Very few problems have only one dimension to them. As a result, one of the best tools for attacking a problem is to break it down into smaller subsets. This is exactly what Wilbur and Orville did when they first addressed the problem of heavier-than-air flight.

Introducing the Tyrant

If you look up the definition of a *tyrant* in the dictionary, you'll see it described as someone (or something) who oppresses in harsh or cruel fashion. During my college days, I remember encountering, on more than a few occasions, a "tyrant" in the form of a final exam. I had a strategy for dealing with it, however. I quickly scanned the test and placed a check mark by all the questions I thought I might have trouble with. Then, believing that it might help "prime the pump," I tackled the easier ones first. By the end of the class, I was facing the hard questions with no time left to answer them. There was little or no chance that I would succeed at the exam. This was exactly the situation the Wright brothers sought to avoid.

> There is no redeeming virtue in putting the tyrant off.

In the problem-solving sense, I define the tyrant as that portion of a problem (i.e., challenge, opportunity, difficulty) that rules, often cruelly, over all other components. It's that part of the problem that, if left unsolved, will prevent solution of the whole. It's the deal breaker, solution buster, worst of the worst. Fail to master this portion of the problem and you cannot possibly, under any set of circumstances, succeed. It is the part of the problem that lurks under the bridge, waiting to attack anyone who attempts to cross it. Please forgive the drama, but I want to make sure everyone understands that the tyrant has the ability to:

» Block, oppress, or impede movement

» Rob individuals of limited resources (i.e., time and money)

» Intimidate, freeze, or otherwise inhibit creativity

» Deceive the problem solver into thinking he is making progress

The principal thing to be understood about the tyrant is that there is no redeeming virtue in putting it off. Doing so can have serious repercussions, causing one to incur significant losses and delays. With everyone understanding that, why do we put off the hardest problem? Why do we work on the easier parts first? There's more than human nature involved.

The Nature of the Beast

Most of us, if pressed for an honest reply, would own up to the tendency of doing the easy things first. Having been bombarded with productivity training and time management seminars, most of us know all about the ABC system. Break your assignments down into A's, B's, and C's, based on the level of importance of each. Start with the "A" stack, and do not do "B" or "C" tasks until all A's are completed. Being the humans that we are, however, we invariably start with something easy in an effort to get something going, especially after a long weekend. Typical reasons why we choose to begin with easier (i.e., nontyrant) components of a problem include:

» It's easy. (Who doesn't like that?)

» It's gratifying. (You get to check a box.)

» It's the area in which we have the greatest knowledge.

➼ It's potentially the most interesting part of the problem.

➼ It conforms best to personal preferences and prejudice.

People may choose to address lesser subsets of a problem because the procrastinator's mind-set may be saying, "It doesn't really matter where you start, just get started!" Poor organizational skills and the inability to manage priorities contribute to this tendency, as well.

There may be other reasons, beyond poor prioritization skills, that may cause us to push nontyrant issues to the head of the list. For example, the boss may want another part of the problem tackled first. Perhaps we choose the nontyrant issues because accomplishing them will look impressive at the next problem status meeting. Or maybe it's just symptomatic of a "we'll cross that bridge when we come to it" mentality.

Identifying the Tyrant

One of the key steps in the Wright brothers' problem-solving process is identifying the tyrant. Here are some of the steps that can be taken to correctly identify it:

➼ Break the problem down into small components, or subsets.

➼ Identify the obstacles and barriers associated with each subset.

➼ Determine the resources (i.e., time, money, people) needed to solve each subset.

➼ Rank subsets in terms of degree of difficulty.

➼ Pick the tyrant.

➼ Tackle the worst (i.e., more difficult) first.

In the problem-solving model of Wilbur and Orville Wright, the tyrant was balance and control. They knew it not only from their studies and preliminary research, but from their work experience as well. Like a bicycle, a flying machine was inherently unstable. Wilbur and Orville knew that if they could provide the means to control and balance a flying machine, gaining the skills needed to fly it would then be possible. Although the

Wright brothers had the problem of flight largely worked out by 1901, it would take another three years of practicing and tweaking of the design to overcome the tyrant. It wasn't until this problem had been resolved that Wilbur and Orville turned their attention to other factors.

The Cost of Ignoring the Tyrant

Ignoring the tyrant in favor of smaller, easier-to-solve portions of the problem can be a costly proposition. Consider, for example, the following penalties of doing so:

- It creates a false sense of security.

- It has many costs (e.g., time and money), the greatest of which is "lost opportunity."

- It compromises speed to market, which is a competitive edge.

- It leads to tunnel vision (i.e., looking only at the areas of the problem you want to see).

- Time loss is doubled, because what you lose, your competitor gains.

- It creates a hiding place for clueless employees.

Let me give you a quick example. A company was suffering through a period of poor sales. The president called his team together and told them, "People, we've got a problem." He went on to tell them that they needed to increase sales (a point they were already well aware of) and that they needed to increase them immediately. After he left, his team brainstormed in an effort to develop new ways to increase sales of their product. When they finished, they had a new sales campaign, a new incentive program for reps, a new volume discount structure, and a new PR program. They were pretty pleased with themselves until one of their service coordinators asked, "Are we going to do anything about the cracking problem?" In one question, she managed to identify the tyrant. Until they resolved the issue of the product's tendency to crack under certain applications, no marketing campaign or sales strategy was going to work. The product, not sales, was the tyrant.

Learning to Soar

Here are some thoughts and ideas to help you identify and tackle the tyrant in your challenge. Remember, if it's easy, do it last. The tyrant, by definition, is the hardest and most potentially unsolvable obstacle you face.

- ↝ *Define your primary objective.* Identifying the tyrant begins with correctly defining the objective. The mistake many people made in addressing the heavier-than-air flying problem was that they defined the problem as "flying." The primary objective of the Wright brothers, the one that led to manned flight, was to fly "balanced and controlled." How the problem is defined can have a huge impact on the end result.

- ↝ *Break the problem down into components.* One of the keys in identifying the tyrant is to see what the potential candidates are. Since most problems have multiple components, begin by breaking the problem down into as many subsets as possible. Consider not only issues directly related to the problem, but also those that might be influenced indirectly by your decisions. For example, the problem may be implementing a new software system. One of its components, however, might be the organization's resistance to change.

- ↝ *Gather as much information as possible.* The first step for the Wright brothers in tackling a problem, or any portion of one, was to find out what was already known—especially what other early aviators had already learned about the problem, or what they had already accomplished. Encourage your team members to gather as much information as possible to correctly assess individual parts of the problem that your organization is confronting. Have them look at your competitors and what they are doing. Don't forget the considerable value of asking others—associates, suppliers, customers, etc.—for their views as well.

- ↝ *Analyze the subsets; identify the obstacles.* Study each component of the problem by asking yourself, What would prevent us from accomplishing this objective? How much time and money and other resources will be needed to solve this component of the problem? What staff (trained and available) will be needed to tackle the challenge? Are there any significant internal issues (e.g., traditions, habits, resistance) that need to be considered? Are there any external hurdles to be overcome in making this work?

➥ *Rank-order the subsets.* Having identified and analyzed the components of the problem, as well as the challenges and obstacles associated with each, begin the process of ranking each, based on the degree of difficulty you might experience in resolving them.

➥ *Identify the tyrant.* Looking at the most difficult subsets, ask yourself which one problem, should it fail to be solved, has the capacity to prevent your team from reaching the defined objective. The tyrant is that portion of the problem that is the hardest and most troublesome to accomplish.

➥ *Tackle the tyrant.* Work on the tyrant and only the tyrant. Resist the temptation to work on some of the easier or more interesting parts first. During the task, ask yourself repeatedly, "Am I working on the tyrant right now?" Failure to do so may result in a significant loss of time, money, and opportunity.

Resist the temptation to tackle jobs you are most comfortable with. Begin with the toughest challenge, one you expect to present the most difficulty. Once the initial tyrant has been resolved, look for the next one.

One Last Thought

A number of years ago I was working with a group of engineers on a product that would subject our parts to high temperature and vibration. Using a high-temp plastic was a standard option that presented no problem. It turned out, however, that the customer wanted us to mold the part in a plastic manufactured by one of its subsidiaries. We knew there was a potential tyrant in the situation, since the shrink rate (i.e., the degree that the material shrinks during the molding process) of the plastics would be different. The mold was designed to work with our plastic, and our customer adamantly refused to pay for a new mold. We needed the business badly, however, and hoped their material would "do okay" in our mold.

In this scenario, we knew exactly what the tyrant was. If the plastic didn't shrink properly in the existing mold, the project was dead. As a result, we set that part of the problem aside and worked on the other design issues (of which there were plenty). We had a great deal of expense—time, money, opportunity, and cost—tied up in this project when we finally reached the critical point. I remember the day our molder called us, spitting nails. Not only had our customer's material failed to meet operating requirements, the plastic had gummed up the molder's dies. It took him four weeks to repair the damage, causing us to not only lose our order, but fall delinquent on orders for other customers as well.

A number of people have asked me why we exposed ourselves to so much risk. The reasons are twofold. First, when you're a smaller company courting a larger one, you often find yourself in situations where you feel you have to take risks. The second reason is what I call the deception of the gradual. We kept working on various parts of the problem hoping we might catch a break at the end. Unfortunately, we came face-to-face with the tyrant at the end, instead of at the beginning, and the costs were enormous—not only to ourselves, but to our customer as well. If we had put the worst first and tackled the tyrant, considerable loss could have been avoided.

CHAPTER FIVE

FIDDLING

THE PRINCIPLE OF INVETERATE TINKERING

Study the science of art and the art of science. Learn how to see and remember that everything is connected to everything else.

Leonardo da Vinci (1452–1519), artist-inventor

FIDDLING is a problem-solving principle that says new ideas and approaches can be created by tinkering with portions of a problem in an effort to understand it, repair it, or make it better. Tinkering, the art of looking for connections and contrasts, can be either conceptual (mental) or tactile (physical). Brainstorming is a form of conceptual tinkering.

*   *   *

Sitting atop a tree-covered hill at the corner of Park and Harmon Avenues in the Dayton suburb of Oakwood, you'll find the majestic home of Orville Wright. The two-story mansion, called Hawthorn Hill, is easily recognized by its classic columns and winding drive. Wilbur and Orville purchased the nineteen-acre site in 1912 and planned to begin construction that fall. The home, to be shared with their sister and father, would be the family's one great indulgence in life. Since Wilbur was heavily involved in the legal battles associated with the defense of their patents, design of the Georgian-style home fell largely to Orville. The work became his alone when Wilbur, stricken with typhoid fever, died several months after the lot was purchased.

Hawthorn Hill is now owned by a Dayton corporation, but it is open for public tours one weekend each fall. The tours, hosted by the Montgomery County Historical Society, give visitors an opportunity to see the mansion largely as it existed in Orville's lifetime. Orville's fingerprints are all over the house, from the in-wall vacuum cleaner system he invented (he didn't want his floors marred by the sweeper) to the showers equipped with circular pipes (he wanted water from all directions). Every need in Orville's mind was an opportunity for tinkering and invention. Not even a hard-to-open mason jar escaped his attention (he invented a special tool for that, too).

Orville loved to solve problems, and he took particular delight in doing so using only the materials on hand.

The highlight of the tour for me, as it is for most people, was Orville's office. Small and book-lined, it has a number of items that remind the visitor of the man's love for fiddling with things. On the arm of his favorite reading chair, for example, sits a device that holds a book open at the proper angle for easy reading. Orville's hands, pained with arthritis, remained free and unstressed. For Orville, tinkering was both a fascination and a challenge. He loved to solve problems, and he took particular delight in doing so using only the materials on hand. As a boy, his penchant for tinkering would help him understand the inner workings of a clock or the treadle of a sewing machine. Later, those skills would be used to perfect the world's first heavier-than-air flying machine.

In the Beginning . . .

In his book, *How We Invented the Airplane*, Orville Wright reveals the "genesis moment" that first inspired the brothers' interest in flying machines. In 1878, Reverend Milton Wright, just appointed a bishop for the United Brethren Church, moved his family to Cedar Rapids, Iowa, to be closer to his assigned territory. Even with the move, he was frequently away on extended trips. Despite a meager $1,000 annual salary, he liked to bring home gifts for his children, especially ones that would challenge their curiosity and increase their knowledge. When he returned from one trip when Wilbur was eleven and Orville seven, the boys jumped up to greet their father, who was holding something behind his back. Before they could reach him, he tossed their gift in the air. Instead of falling to the floor, their present hovered near the ceiling for a minute, then settled to the ground. Their curiosity piqued, the boys quickly picked it up and began examining the little flying machine made of cork, wood, and cardboard.

The gift Bishop Wright brought his sons that day in 1878 was a toy helicopter of the type designed by a Frenchman named Alphonse Pénaud (1850–1880). Although toy flying machines had been around for nearly a century, Pénaud's models were unique in that they featured two propellers powered by a twisted rubber band (earlier models were powered by a bow and bowstring). Orville recounts that the brothers quickly wore the toy out, then began tinkering with it in an attempt to make it better. Later, they tried to make larger versions, but they were unable to get them to fly. It would be years before the brothers would understand the exponential relationship between size and power (a machine twice the size of the original requires eight times as much power). Nevertheless, the Pénaud helicopter would remain in the back of their minds for years to come.

What Goes Around Comes Around

Alphonse Pénaud's influence on the Wright brothers would be felt again when they began to seriously consider the challenge of heavier-than-air flight in 1899. Pénaud, a French marine engineer and son of an admiral, had planned a career in the navy. His plans were dashed by a degenerative hip disease that left him confined to a wheelchair. Looking for other outlets for his considerable skills, Pénaud turned his attention to flying machines. Influenced by the English aerial pioneer Sir George Cayley, Pénaud began experimenting with models. To finance his work, he began selling some of his models as toys. One of those toys ended up in the hands of two impressionable young boys in America.

Pénaud was making great strides with his models, creating an effective means of establishing equilibrium. The wings on his models formed a dihedral angle, which, when combined with a rear stabilizer (i.e., tail fin), allowed them to maintain stability in flight. Unable to raise the funds needed to create full-size versions of his models (the French government had rebuffed his requests), a despondent Pénaud took his life in 1880 at the age of twenty-nine. Pénaud's work would be studied in great detail by aviation pioneers Otto Lilienthal and Octave Chanute, as well as the Wright brothers. All would incorporate some of Pénaud's features into their designs. Pénaud, who would become known as the "father of flying models," died feeling he had failed to contribute to the flying problem.

Fiddling Around

Although there's anecdotal evidence that each of the brothers loved fiddling with things, Pénaud's toy helicopter may offer the first evidence of Wilbur and Orville tinkering in tandem. Both men were blessed with insatiable curiosities, hungry to understand how things worked. Consider the following episodes during their youth:

- By age five, Orville is tinkering with clocks, taking them apart and correctly putting them back together again. A neighbor's mother complains how hard it is to get oil into a tiny hole in her sewing machine. Orville finds the solution to this problem by dipping a feather into the oil, then letting it drip off the tip into the hole.

- At age ten, Orville takes up the sport of kite flying. He develops ways to make his kites lighter and stronger (a skill that will come in handy later), then begins selling them to other kids. Wilbur is also interested, but he refrains from participating for fear of looking juvenile.

- When Wilbur is fourteen and Orville ten, they decide to build a wooden lathe similar to one they had seen in their grandfather's barn. Unhappy with the vibration it creates, they tinker with it until they find a solution. Metal rings, removed from an old harness hanging in the barn, are combined with clay marbles to fashion ball bearings to make the shaft turn more smoothly.

➬ Soon after the lathe project, Orville notices that many of the kids in his school have taken up chewing pieces of tar. Thinking that flavoring might make the tar more appealing, he begins working with ingredients to make the tar sweeter. Years later Wilbur would kid his brother by making reference to that "chawin' gum corporation."

➬ At age twelve, Orville reads an article on woodcutting in *Century Magazine*. He studies everything he can find (always a starting point) on the subject at the library, then begins fiddling with materials to make the tools he needs. He fashions an engraving tool from the hardened-steel spring of an old pocketknife that allows him to make accurate cuts. He uses his father's cider-type letterpress to apply the pressure needed to transfer the pattern from woodcut to paper.

➬ At age sixteen, Orville's interest in printing has grown from hobby to business. Needing a better printing press, but not having the money to buy one, he improvises. He creates a cost-effective press using scrap iron and wood scavenged from a backyard lumber pile.

➬ When a friend shows Orville a new adding machine his company is using, Orville finds the machine's eighty-one keys too complicated to use. He experiments a bit and produces a ten-key model that not only adds and subtracts, it multiplies. He then reworks a noisy typewriter, greatly improving its operation by making it less complicated.

➬ When the Wright brothers need a wind tunnel to test the lift and drag of various wing shapes, they make it out of an old soapbox and the drive shaft of a discarded grinder. The balances inside are fashioned out of bicycle spokes and old hacksaw blades. Their "tinkered" solution allows them to disprove the validity of research data relied upon by experimenters for over a century.

> For the Wright brothers, tinkering was how they examined the interrelatedness of things.

Fiddling, Fame, and Fortune

As you examine the work of the Wright brothers throughout the years they were actively working on the problem of manned flight, you'll notice that fiddling with things and ideas was a key component of their problem-solving process. Their penchant for constantly tinkering with something in an effort to first learn and understand, then repair or improve it, is the thread that weaves itself through everything they did, from the design of a wind tunnel to the shape and placement of a rudder. For the Wright brothers, tinkering was how they examined the interrelatedness of things, and this enabled them to break the incredibly complex task of building a heavier-than-air flying machine down into manageable components.

Hands Working in Concert

A strong case can be made that tinkering brought the famed Wright brothers partnership into being. Orville's interest in printing had been growing ever since his woodcutting days. He had owned and operated several small presses, but in 1888, at the age of seventeen, he wanted a larger press for bigger jobs. Without the money to buy one, he began laying out his own version. Once it began to take shape in his thoughts, just like a flying machine would years later, he began to picture what was needed to make it work. Orville relied on his own resourcefulness. "The gap between resource and opportunity," writes Mark Bernstein in *Grand Eccentrics,* "was patched over with improvisation and invention."

A natural scavenger, Orville hit all the local junkyards and accumulated a selection of odds and ends. Lumber was expensive, so he rounded up some firewood that worked just as well. A hard surface was required, so Orville visited a local mortuary and purchased a used gravestone. When he needed a way to apply even, repetitive pressure to the type for the imprint, Orville went to the barn behind his house and began looking for something that might work. He noticed the collapsing mechanism on an old family buggy and soon had it removed and in place on his printing press. It was close to working, but a few nagging problems seemed to be beyond his grasp. It turned out to be a very fortunate lapse.

Wilbur, at age twenty-one, was going through a period of trying to find himself. After suffering a serious injury in a hockey game when he was eighteen, he had slipped into a state of melancholy that would last several years. Watching Orville work on his press, Wilbur noticed his brother had reached an impasse. With a mind full of ideas of how the machine might be made to work, he offered his assistance to Orville as a consultant. Tinkering in tandem, the two men were able to come up with a design that defied logic, but worked perfectly. It was the first time the brothers had worked together to solve a significant problem. Their capacity to fiddle with something until a solution emerged would be an asset right up to the moment Orville eased their *Wright Flyer* into the sky. It would even help solve a problem that, just days before that flight, threatened to forestall it.

The Just-in-Case Box

In August 1903, the Wright brothers were "good to go and ready to launch." By the end of their 1902 season at Kill Devil Hills, they had worked out most of the issues related to balance and control. During the following spring and summer, they completed work on a lightweight motor and two "pusher type" propellers. As they were preparing to head to the Outer Banks of North Carolina, the brothers began chucking an odd assortment of items into a "just-in-case box." Wright biographer Fred Howard describes the stuff as a "motley collection of odds and ends from the bicycle shop." Among the items chucked into the crate were bicycle hubs, carbide cans, assorted tools, and a tube of Arnstein's hard tire cement. The items in the box had no predetermined use. They were included, along with other essential items, to give the brothers some raw materials to work with should some serious tinkering be necessary. It was.

The brothers were working feverishly in November 1903, ever mindful that Samuel Langley's flying machine was close to completion. A number of nagging problems had plagued their efforts, but by November 5, their flyer was ready to go. Then, during a test run, excessive vibration caused by the slapping and jerking of the chain drive badly damaged one of the propeller shafts. Repairing the shafts was a job only Charlie Taylor, the Wright brothers' mechanic at their shop in Dayton, could do. The shafts were shipped to Taylor on the fifth of November and returned to the brothers on the seventeenth. The new shafts were immediately mounted on the flyer and subjected to a test run. The run was so rough, the sprocket wheels worked loose. Try as they might, no amount of tightening would resolve the issue. Late in the evening the brothers gave up on the problem and headed to bed, disgusted with the whole mess. Although frustrated and discouraged with the turn of events, Wilbur and Orville continued to think and debate the problem with the sprockets. They were still tinkering, but were now doing it conceptually. Their minds served as a comfortable workshop. By dawn a solution was playing inside Orville's head. One of the items in their motley collection of stuff hauled down from Dayton "just in case" was a tube of Arnstein's cement, a product the men used in their bicycle business to seal tires to rims. The glue had once been used by the brothers to repair a watch a clockmaker had deemed irreparable. The cement was quickly located, heated up so it would flow, then poured over the sprocket threads. Once the cement set, the problem of the loose sprocket wheel was solved. Again, they had tinkered their way to a solution. It worked then, and it works today. Let me share an example.

Square Pegs in Round Holes

A company I worked for years ago manufactured electronic connectors, including a product commonly known as a "header." Computer users may remember these parts as the ones jumpers were placed on to change functions. The pins in the header had square tails to accommodate a method of attachment used decades earlier called "wire wrapping." Later, when wave soldering became popular, connector companies continued to make square-tailed parts (traditions are hard to break). To make the part easier to place on the printed circuit board and solder more efficiently, our company developed tooling that would coin the tail. The result was a part with rounded, rather than square tails.

One day we received a call from an engineer with a huge problem. He had just received a shipment of 50,000 printed circuit boards with connector holes that failed to meet design specifications. The square-tailed parts he had purchased from a competitor wouldn't fit, and he didn't have time to rework the boards. Unless his company completed and shipped assemblies to the customer in three days, it stood to lose an important account. "I was fiddling around with your parts with the coined tail," he told me, "and discovered that yours fit where the others don't." It seems that by coining the corners of our parts, we removed just enough material to compensate for the error in the board. This engineer's tinkering saved his company time and money, plus an important customer. It also netted us a nice order. Tinkering works.

Tinkering and the Psychology of LEGOs

In the early 1900s, when toy maker Charles Pajeau was looking for a new concept, he noticed that children loved to play with the empty thread spools left over after the thread had been used up. Combined with homemade sticks, they provided hours of entertainment for imaginative kids. Pajeau took the idea, fiddled with it, and introduced Tinkertoys at the 1914 New York Toy Fair. The product was an instant hit. Building on the popularity of the build-it-yourself toy craze, John Lloyd Wright (son of Frank Lloyd Wright) introduced Lincoln Logs. The principle at work in these toys, as well as the Erector Sets of A. C. Gilbert, was largely the same: Create the resources and let the child's imagination take over. Although all three of these creativity-enhancing toys came with instructions on how to build set models, the vast amount of creations produced were the original conceptions of the child. Although each set contained directions, kids quickly abandoned them in favor of their own imaginative designs.

There's no doubt the Wright brothers would have loved Erector Sets, Tinkertoys, and Lincoln Logs. They would have especially loved LEGO kits, those colorful building blocks that interlock to form various designs. My guess is that the first thing the brothers would want to understand is the principle of force distribution that holds the blocks together. This creative toy challenges the user to fiddle with the parts until something emerges from the pile. Various shapes, sizes, and colors give the user thousands of options in his creative effort. The possibilities are endless, as Jim Sato illustrates in *LEGO Mindstorms*, his popular book on LEGO use. As dedicated fiddlers, I bet the Wright brothers would have worn out their sets in no time, perhaps even developed a better version.

Tinker Types

Whenever I'm hired to facilitate a visioning session or to lead a group through a problem-solving exercise, I come armed with a bucket full of LEGOs. Sometimes I'll just dump the parts in a pile in the center of the table and let the people have at it. Other times, I'll give each participant her own bag (all bags having the same parts) and urge everyone to create something while we're brainstorming for ideas. I remember one session when someone stated, "I can't do both things (think and create) at once!" Responses to the assignment often reveal a lot about the individual, and possibly even his company. Over the years, as I've observed people during the tinkering assignment, I've created four categories to describe the tinkering styles of different people. They are:

- *Taskers*. These are the people who assemble their parts quickly, usually in a block or unintelligible mass. Once their creation is assembled, they set it aside where it remains untouched until the program concludes. In their mind, they have succeeded because they completed the task given to them.

- *Conformists*. These are the people who put their parts together often in unique and creative ways. Once they see someone else's creation, however, they revise theirs to bring it into conformance with those of their peers.

- *Averters*. These individuals are more concerned with avoiding a risk than they are with creating something. The risk they're most concerned about is the possibility that they might appear silly or foolish. Their bag of building blocks remains untouched until the end of the program, at which time they ask, "Can I take these home for the kids?"

- *Visionaries*. These people never leave their blocks alone. Over the course of the seminar, they will change their creations repeatedly. It's not uncommon to find them making final "tweaks" as the program concludes.

Although I didn't give them a name, I have a fifth group as well. These are the people who do nothing with their pile. They describe the exercise as "silly" and refuse to play. Leaving this group unnamed is, in reality, its best description.

Priming the (Tinkering) Pump

I recently facilitated a planning session for the board of trustees of a non-profit agency. As instructed, the board members fiddled with their building blocks throughout the program. At the end of the day, I asked each person to show the group his creation. The assortment of objects shown demonstrated incredible creativity! As people showed their creations and volunteered explanations, the energy of the group rose accordingly. There was laughter, there was praise, and there were a large number of "solutions." Although everyone had started out with the same number, size, and color blocks, no two creations were alike. A number of people asked if they could take their models back to the office as reminders of the principle demonstrated.

As the former "Dean of Disneyland," Mike Vance is in great demand as a creative-thinking consultant. Vance often recommends companies develop a "creative center" on-site where employees can go to be inspired. He suggests stocking it with books and tapes of all types to stimulate thinking. I like Vance's idea, but I would fill the room with creative toys as well. Give employees thirty minutes on their own with a LEGO kit or an Erector Set, and I'll bet they'll learn more about the creative process than they would flipping through books on the subject. If you'd prefer an exercise with more structure, contact the LEGO Company directly. It offers a two-day executive seminar on how to use its plastic blocks as a strategic tool. It costs $10,000, but you get to keep the fifty pounds of LEGOs when it's over.

Three Kinds of Tinkering

Tinkering, by definition, is the process of fiddling with something in an effort to understand it, repair it, or make it better. I like to break tinkering into three categories, or methods: tangible tinkering, conceptual tinkering, and hybrid tinkering. Generally speaking, all three methods are activated to some degree by the presence of a problem or an opportunity. Sometimes that problem is the sole subject of the thought process. Other times, tinkering might have an impact on a problem or opportunity running concurrently in the background. The benefits of tinkering as a problem-solving tool include the following:

- It can be used effectively as an individual or group exercise.

- It helps to incubate undeveloped ideas.

- It teaches people to use all tools (physical and mental) in the creative process.

- It maximizes the creative principle of invention-extension.

- It gives the individual ownership of the thinking process.

- It can occur anytime, anyplace.

- It shifts the mind-set of the employee from tasks to outcomes.

Any time someone tinkers with an idea or a tangible item, there is the potential for that person to improve on it. Let's take a closer look at the tinkering categories—tactile, conceptual, and hybrid—and how each might be applied to problem solving.

Tactile Tinkering

Tinkering, as previously noted, is the act of looking at something with an eye to figuring it out or making it better. For the Wright brothers, tinkering often involved a problem with a tangible item. It's not hard to picture Orville standing at the workbench in his shop apron and sleeve cuffs thoughtfully considering some mechanical challenge. He'd be fiddling with some gear or sprocket, turning it over and over, looking for some insight or connection. He might look at it for a while in its most logical sense, then begin asking himself a series of "what if" questions. What if I reverse this process? What if I make it larger (or smaller, longer, shorter, etc.)? It was in this fashion that the brothers developed an oil-retaining hub and improved coaster brakes for the bicycles they made. Orville engaged in a process that I call tactile tinkering, the act of applying physical senses (e.g., sight, touch, smell) to a tangible item.

My father was one of the best tactile tinkerers I ever knew. As a minister's family, we were often short of money. As a result, if anything broke—toaster, bicycle, lawnmower—Dad would repair it using whatever was at hand. The key part of his creative process was poking around in his catchall drawer for something that looked or felt like it might, with a bit of tweaking, do the job. One of his most memorable tinkering projects involved the bathroom faucet that was clogged at the spout. Unable to clear it, he removed the part to replace it.

When told it would be several weeks before the part would be available, he took a metal measuring cup and secured it in place with some thick rubber bands. On the surface, it doesn't sound too impressive, but the cup deflected the water coming out of the stem, directing it into the sink. The person using the faucet could grasp the cup by its handle and direct the flow of water wherever desired. The rubber bands provided just enough tension to keep the flow pointed in one direction until the handle was moved. As I look back from the distance of four decades, I realize my dad was on the verge of inventing the single-levered faucet so popular today.

Conceptual Tinkering

One morning, while working on their flyer in Kitty Hawk, Orville announced that during the night he had solved a problem regarding the control of their machine. "I was lying awake last night," Orville said, "and I studied out a new vertical, movable rudder to replace the fixed rudder we have used." Orville's ability to visualize a solution would be a key component of the brothers' eventual success, one that would allow them to control the direction of the flight path (yaw). In terms of importance, it was at least as significant as Wilbur's wing-warping concept (discussed later). Many experts on the Wright brothers feel that their ability to "see" things in their heads before they tangibly existed was one of their greatest assets. I call it conceptual tinkering.

Conceptual tinkering has no tangible component. This creative process takes place entirely in what is commonly called the mind's eye. As such, it can occur anytime and at any place. I once worked with an engineer who went to the YMCA every day at lunch to swim. When he returned, he'd come into my office and say, "I've had an idea about how we might . . . ." If you asked him where his creativity came from, he'd say the act of swimming stimulated him. While this might be true on some level, the real answer was that he had a block of time each day dedicated to mental tinkering. Companies that emphasize tasks over outcomes do not challenge (or make provision for) employees to really think.

Hybrid Tinkering

Wilbur Wright was working in his bicycle shop one day when a customer came in to purchase an inner tube. While talking with the customer, Wilbur began fiddling with the cardboard box the tube had come in. As he twisted it in his hands, he noticed how the top and bottom of the box behaved when he rotated it. In his mind, he could picture the same effect on the double-deck wings of a flying machine. Using both conceptual and tangible tinkering, he saw a solution to lateral control that everyone else had missed. It was a solution without which controlled flight would have been impossible. His solution remains in use today, a hundred years later.

Wilbur and his inner tube box are a perfect example of what I call hybrid tinkering. When he was mindlessly twisting the box, Wilbur was engaged in tangible activity. He was holding it in his hands (tactility), twisting it (motion), and observing it (sight). To this, however, he added his ability to tinker conceptually by projecting his tactile experience onto the problem of controlling a flying machine. The combination of tactile and conceptual tinkering results in a powerful creative tool. Hybrid tinkering is about merging the senses (seeing, feeling, touching, smelling) with the imagination to create new possibilities and connections.

> Using both conceptual and tangible tinkering, Wilbur saw a solution to lateral control that everyone else had missed.

A Lost Art

What was once regarded as an American strength seems to have fallen on hard times. A meeting several years ago with a vice president of marketing illustrates my point. While we were talking, he wanted to pull some data off his computer. When he went to print the information, the paper jammed the printer. He tried to pull it loose, then gave up. "I'll send it to you later," he said. I told him that we could probably remove the back of the printer and get at the jammed paper. "Don't worry," he said, "we have people we pay to do that sort of thing." The solution to the problem, in this fellow's eyes, was to issue a work order for someone else to fix it, or to just buy a new printer. His justification was that his time was not worth expending on a menial task like clearing a jammed printer. The problem is, when called upon to demonstrate real creativity, as marketing people are often expected to do, a key problem-solving skill—tinkering—may be severely underdeveloped.

In his book *Brain Power,* Karl Albrecht noted that Americans seem to prefer a passive experience to an active one when it comes to learning to think creatively. "With the ability to trade their money for solutions to the various logistical problems of living," he said, "Americans may be losing their ability to solve problems, to innovate, to improvise, and to repair." In the two decades since Albrecht penned those words, things may have gotten worse. The reasons for this reluctance run the gamut, from "That's not my job" to "I never was very good at things like that."

Regardless of the reason, companies today are staffed with people unfamiliar with the concept of tinkering to learn, understand, repair, or improve. Instead of viewing it as a form of creativity, many employees have been taught that fiddling is an expression of idleness, a waste of time. If something breaks, buy another one. If an idea doesn't fit, discard it. If a project gets bogged down, abandon it. You have to wonder what would have happened to the *Apollo 13* spacecraft when it suffered an explosion in deep space if it had been filled with such individuals.

One of the most exciting scenes in the movie *Apollo 13* occurs when the engineers at ground control have to develop a solution to a critical filtering problem on the spacecraft. One of the men walks in with a box full of odds and ends and says, "This is what they have available on the capsule." The engineers were given a limited amount of time to tinker with the items until they found a solution. Using a creative skill most had probably acquired as kids, they fashioned a device that saved three lives, not to mention the future of NASA. What response would this type of challenge generate in your company?

Learning to Soar

Remember, fiddling is not a mindless exercise, but the art of making connections, comparisons, and contrasts. Tinkering—tactile, conceptual, or hybrid—should be a part of every company's problem-solving strategy. Here are a few tips to make the process effective in your organization.

> *Give staff the freedom to look foolish.* Giving your team members the freedom to look silly or foolish, without risking ridicule or reprisal, frees them to consider ideas and approaches that might otherwise go unexplored. One way to encourage this is to sponsor "wildest idea" contests. At worst, participants will be energized by the laugher and enthusiasm it creates. At best, they'll be excited by the generation of ideas and possibilities previously unseen. The idea is to allow the "fiddler's" mind to go wherever it might take him. Invention-extension, which involves taking a "silly" idea and using it as a springboard to a viable one, is best served by returning to the source of those ideas—creative tinkering.

> **Fiddling is not a mindless exercise, but the art of making connections, comparisons, and contrasts.**

> *Discourage milk runs.* Getting in the habit of doing things the same way is often a detriment to creativity. As the old saying goes, if you always do what you've always done, you'll always get what you've always got. I call this approach a milk run because it involves making the same stops on the same route every day. Since creative tinkering works best when powered by an active curiosity, consider rewarding employees bold enough to look for alternative paths.

> *Scrounge, forage, and rummage.* Tinkerers need raw materials, tangible and intangible, to work with. Wright biographer Fred Howard describes Orville as a "gifted scrounger," adept at mental and physical foraging. He was referring to Orville's ability to search everywhere for available ideas and materials. Previous experience or personal bias would not deter him from looking in new areas. Challenge your employees to look for opportunities (i.e., ideas) everywhere. Drive time, long walks at lunch hour, daily swims—all can be restructured as scrounging opportunities.

➥ *Look at problems from as many angles as possible.* The process of tinkering requires the item under consideration to be examined from as many directions as possible. Turn it over. Turn it inside out. Look for connections, similarities, or contrasts. Resist the need to be logical or make sense. Ask the question a different way. Once you get the first "right" answer, look for two or three more.

➥ *Encourage tactile tinkering by creating a tinkering room.* Create a place where staff members can go and do some tactile tinkering. Encourage them to take a few minutes to play with tinkering tools (e.g., LEGO kits, Erector Sets, etc.) and get comfortable with the creative principles they imply. Encourage employees to apply the same tactics to the problem they're seeking to solve by looking for connections or interrelatedness.

➥ *Fiddle first, ask questions later.* Just as in brainstorming sessions, the objective is to bring forth as many ideas as possible without allowing our built-in judge to disqualify them. Again, the process of invention-extension, using one idea as inspiration for another, is a key element in this problem-solving principle. Fiddling is the art of following leads, ideas, and hunches wherever they might take you without worrying about established rules and norms.

➥ *Encourage people to really think.* Original thinking, the process whereby we consider something first from our own unique perspective before seeking the views of others, is rare. Tinkering may be powered by curiosity, but it's best expressed in original thought. Encourage employees to ask themselves on a regular basis, "What is my unique perspective on this subject?"

The Wright brothers were inveterate tinkerers. It was a habitual, life-long practice that would influence their work throughout their careers. Activated by an insatiable curiosity nurtured by their father and fueled by their mother's mechanical aptitude, Wilbur and Orville would spend a lifetime looking at everything around them with an eye to understanding it, then seeing if there was a way to do things better. Tinkering was a key component of their problem-solving model, one that can be applied today as well.

One Last Thought

In 1986, I was in Japan to meet with a group of businessmen hired to distribute my company's products. Our first meeting together had been a get-acquainted session that involved remarkably little conversation. Even though I understood the first meeting was meant to "get a feel" for each other, the nonproductivity of the session (time is money) was driving me nuts. After several hours, the meeting was concluded. As I gathered my materials to leave, the handle on my briefcase broke, causing it to hit the table—then the floor—with a thud. The look on the faces of my hosts conveyed their sympathy that such a great embarrassment had befallen me. I fully expected someone to offer me the proverbial ceremonial sword.

As I examined my briefcase, I determined that a stud on the handle had sheared off. I noticed a paper clip on the table, so I used it to fashion a temporary repair. As I was doing this, I was surprised to see a dozen of the businessmen pressed around me like medical students witnessing an operation in a hospital amphitheater. Little "oohs" and "aahs" could be heard as I fished the extended paper clip through the handle, rejoining it to the case. I used a fingernail cutter in my pocket to twist the ends and then trim them off. As I finished, I gave the case a couple of jerks to see if it was going to hold. It did. The men, to whom the concept of tinkering was alien, gave me a polite round of applause. I think Wilbur and Orville would have been pleased.

CHAPTER SIX

MIND-WARPING

THE PRINCIPLE OF RIGID FLEXIBILITY

Great artists, scientists, and spiritual masters lead humanity forward by diverging from dominant paradigms, blending imaginative vision with reason and practicality.

Michael Gelb, *Thinking for a Change*

MIND-WARPING is a problem-solving principle that encourages flexing the mind, allowing it to consider possibilities that fall outside the plane of thought established (and limited) by policy, tradition, and personal experience. It is the ability to think "outside the box," without abandoning the box.

*   *   *

After their first season of gliding at Kitty Hawk in 1900, the Wright brothers returned home bruised but optimistic. Although their experiments with their glider had been filled with some anxious moments, Wilbur and Orville were encouraged. Later, Wilbur noted that they considered it quite an achievement to "return home without having our pet theories completely knocked in the head by the hard logic of experience." There were no short-ages of pet theories in aeronautics research in 1900, and most of them were, literally and figuratively, getting "knocked in the head."

Chauffeurs and Airmen

Aviation owes a debt of gratitude to British historian Sir Charles Gibbs-Smith. Gibbs-Smith, who died in 1981, devoted a good portion of his life to recording the early history of aeronautics, particularly the contribution of the Wright brothers. In framing aviation's story, Gibbs-Smith found it useful to classify those address-ing the heavier-than-air flying problem according to the philosophical approach of the experi-menter. Those who thought that power and propulsion were the keys to manned flight were placed in a category Gibbs-Smith called chauffeurs. Those who believed piloting and control were the key issues were called airmen.

> They were able to see the problem, but only as one might "see" the pattern of a tapestry by viewing it from the backside.

Gibbs-Smith chose the term "chauffeur" for the power and propulsion group because it effectively described what these experimenters expected to happen once they were able to get their machines airborne. Simply stated, they thought that once in the air, their flying machines could be "driven," much as one would drive a car or steer a boat. These pioneers saw their crafts as "ships of the air" that could be made to rise, descend, or turn simply by moving a rudder up or down, left or right. The concept of controlling their flyers along three axes—pitch, roll, and yaw—was a problem yet to be addressed.

When viewed from a distance of a hundred years, the chauffeur approach to manned flight seems inconceivable. In 1900, however, the secrets of flight remained well hidden. Proponents of power and propul-sion, the "chauffeurs" Gibbs-Smith describes, included some of the brightest scientists and engineers of the day. To these flying-machine pio-neers, the "plane of air" was just another highway to drive on. The focus of their efforts, consequently, was on the power needed to generate suffi-cient propulsion to get their machines off the ground. The "rest" could be worked out later.

Most notable among the chauffeurs were Hiram Maxim, inventor of the Maxim machine gun; Clément Ader, the French communications pioneer; and Professor Samuel Pierpont Langley, the head of the Smithsonian Institution. Maxim and Ader were strong proponents of power and propulsion. Langley got there by default. He initially identified control and balance as the key issues, but found himself unable to pull away from his efforts to build a successful motor. "Few men," Tom Crouch notes in *The Bishop's Boys,* "possess the imagination or insight to break the traditional mode of thinking." To some degree, the personal prejudices of all three men toward their points of view kept them from being able to frame the problem in terms of anything other than their own experience. They were able to see the problem, but only as one might "see" the pattern of a tapestry by viewing it from the backside.

Airmen

The other category Gibbs-Smith created was that of "airmen." These experimenters believed that the key to flight was the ability to pilot and control the craft. Airmen were those pioneers who sought to uncover the secrets of balance and control by conducting gliding experiments. These intrepid souls climbed time and again to the top of hills and sand dunes—even buildings—and flung themselves off them in an effort to discover how a flying machine behaves. The solution to the problem, they believed, lay in making as many glides as possible to learn the art of flying. Over a period of five years, one airman, Otto Lilienthal, would make more than 2,000 glides. The Wright brothers would make half that many glides in two months.

Those who fell in the airmen category were later broken into two additional groups based on their approach to the concept of aircraft stability. Octave Chanute (1832–1910), among others, felt that the primary objective of experimenters should be to develop methods for eliminating instability. The focus of this group was on developing the automatic systems needed to correct the machine's wayward movements. The second group, represented primarily by the Wright brothers, believed that the key was to *conquer* the inherent instability of a flying machine by providing means to control and balance it. Instead of trying to eliminate the instability inherent in the craft, the goal was to preserve it and give the operator the means to overcome it.

Inherent Instability

To understand the heavier-than-air flying problem the Wright brothers faced, it's important to understand the concept of inherent instability. In 1900, a flying machine at best was an erratic and unstable craft. Yet not everyone trying to solve the problem understood this. In a speech to the Western Society of Engineers in August 1901, Wilbur used a piece of paper to illustrate the vagaries (i.e., inherent instability) of a flying machine:

> If I take this piece of paper and, after placing it parallel with the ground, quickly let it fall, it will not settle down as a staid, sensible piece of paper ought to do, but it insists in contravening every recognized rule of decorum, turning over and darting hither and thither in the most erratic manner, much after the style of an untrained horse. Yet this is the style of steed that men must learn to manage before flying can become an everyday sport.

The best way to understand inherent instability is to do what Wilbur did: Hold a piece of paper parallel to the floor and let it drop. If you want to really appreciate the concept, picture yourself as a little pilot sitting on that piece of paper trying to control it! The paper's erratic behavior, darting in whatever direction it chooses, was, in the opinion of Wilbur and Orville, the problem of flight itself. Not everyone agreed.

It was only natural that the Wright brothers would fall in the airmen/inherent instability category since, as bicycle builders, they were more than a little familiar with the concepts of balance and control. When a person learns to ride a bicycle, the experience is initially unsettling. In short order, however, the rider learns to balance the bicycle (keep it upright) and control it (direct its path). They also knew the inherent instability of a bicycle could be overcome with the proper combination of human skill and superior design. The Wright brothers, who now understood this was the problem of flight itself, focused their efforts on developing a means to maintain lateral equilibrium. The problem was how to do it without risking the life of the pilot.

> The Wright brothers knew that lateral control was not only a challenging problem, it was a potentially fatal one as well.

A Dangerous Profession

In the aeronautics context, lateral equilibrium is the ability to keep the wings of an aircraft level. The pilot must be able to make a series of adjustments that counteract the vagaries of nature. Early aviation pioneers attempted to do this manually by shifting their weight in flight. Lilienthal, the German glider expert, controlled his gliders by swinging his legs, which dangled freely below his craft, to shift weight. John Montgomery, the first American to conduct successful glides, and Percy Pilcher, a Brit, used similar approaches. By 1900, Pilcher and Lilienthal had lost their lives in gliding accidents when they lost control of their crafts. Montgomery would suffer a similar fate a few years later. The Wright brothers knew that lateral control was not only a challenging problem, but a potentially fatal one as well.

When the Wrights first identified control and balance as the "tyrant" (see Chapter 4), they knew that giving the operator as much control as possible over his craft was an essential part of the solution. They knew that automatic stability was not only unachievable (at that time), but unnecessary. They knew from their experience in cycling that if the means of controlling and balancing their flying machine was available, then the problem of inherent instability could be overcome through operator skill. The challenge, of course, was how to give the operator that ability without killing him in the process.

A Starting Point

I spent a week on the Outer Banks of North Carolina gathering information for my book. One morning, in an effort to duplicate some Wright brothers research, I took my coffee outside and spent an hour watching birds in flight, just as Wilbur and Orville had done a century earlier. Before long, I was treated to the sight of two hawks gliding majestically across a cloudless Atlantic sky. At times they appeared to be suspended in the air, almost coming to a stop. As I watched the birds, I paid particular attention to the tips of their wings. Wilbur shared his observations on this phenomenon in a letter to Octave Chanute in May 1900:

> My observation of the flight of buzzards leads me to believe that they regain their lateral balance, when partly overturned by a gust of wind, by a torsion of the tips of the wings. If the rear edge of the

right wing tip is twisted upward and the left downward, the bird becomes an animated windmill and instantly begins a turn, a line from head to tail, being the axis.

The Wright brothers figured if they could discover a way to build flexibility into wing design, they could make their flyer controllable. It was, as Wilbur later described it, "a conceptual leap of incredible consequence." The challenge was how to create that motion, to flex the tips of their flyer like the birds did.

The Wright brothers' approach to the problem was later detailed by Orville in *How We Invented the Airplane*. "The first method that occurred to us for maintaining lateral equilibrium," he wrote, "was that of pivoting the wings on the right and left sides on shafts." Orville's original concept featured a set of gears in the middle of the flyer that would mesh, causing one wing to rotate upward when the opposite was rotated downward. By this method, he believed that balance could be achieved without the need to constantly shift weight. Although the idea looked good on paper, it brought the Wright brothers face-to-face with two needs that appeared to be mutually exclusive.

Wing-Warping

The Wright brothers discovered that while they needed the wings of their flyer to be *flexible* (for control), they had an equally great need for them to be *rigid* (for support). These needs—rigidity and flexibility—seemed incompatible and unachievable. As Orville noted, they saw no way of building a device that would be strong enough to support the craft yet light enough to actually use. It was a dilemma that, if not resolved, would end their efforts to solve the problem of manned flight. The answer came a short time later when Wilbur, while fiddling with an empty inner tube box (see Chapter 5), conceived the concept of wing torsioning.

Torsioning is the act of twisting an object by applying equal pressure in opposite directions to each end. When Wilbur twisted the inner tube box, which retained its rigidity while being flexed, he immediately saw that the same principle could be transferred to the wings of a flying machine. In terms of historical impact, Wilbur's inner tube box is at least as important as Isaac Newton's apple. He and Orville immediately designed and built a large kite to test the theory. Orville was not present the day Wilbur flew their kite, but he received an enthusiastic report of its success later from his brother. Within a few months of taking up the problem, the Wright brothers had already solved one of its most challenging issues. The torsioning concept would later be called "wing-warping" by Octave Chanute, a term the Wright brothers would adopt as well.

Wing-warping provided the Wright brothers with a solution that most others regarded as unachievable. Their design, called a trussed-biplane, featured two wings one on top of the other, separated with wooden spars. To solve this portion of the flying problem, the brothers understood the need to preserve *both* elements. One element (rigidity) did not need to be sacrificed to the other one (flexibility); in fact, the two actually functioned in a synergistic relationship. The compatibility of two seemingly mutually exclusive forces yielded not only a solution to flight, but a problem-solving principle that can be broadly applied today in many situations.

Mind-Warping

In many respects, what the Wright brothers were trying to create in their flying machine—namely, rigid flexibility—was representative of one of the problem-solving principles they used to secure it. As meticulous professionals, the Wright brothers would have had difficulty discarding the need to think structurally, carefully considering established "truths." At the same time, however, they were flexible enough to consider options that lay "outside the box." Playing off the term used to describe the Wright brothers' method of securing lateral equilibrium, I like to represent the problem-solving principle of rigid flexibility by the term *mind-warping*. I define it as follows:

Mind-warping is the act of flexing the mind, allowing it to consider possibilities that fall outside the plane of thought established (and limited) by rules, traditions, and personal experience. It is the ability to:

➹ Approach a problem logically, while seriously considering illogical options

•→ Move seamlessly back and forth between the abstract and the concrete

•→ Think outside the box, without abandoning the box

Although the benefits of the problem-solving principle of mind-warping are numerous, its primary value is allowing the user to mentally "soar" without giving up the "safety net."

The human mind likes to stay on an even plane (i.e., follow a line of thought). Once flexed, a number of forces are counterexerted to push it back into "proper" alignment. Some of the forces exerting pressure include prior experience, personal bias (habit), professional training, and education and culture (traditions). Understanding that these forces are at work is the first step in preparing ourselves to use the principle of rigid flexibility.

Chained by Our Certitudes

I have a nice collection of tools in my workshop, including a half dozen claw hammers. I use only one of them, though, a wooden-handled beauty I've had for years. There's nothing unique about it. I just like the way it feels. It's comfortable and familiar, with just enough wear to conform nicely to the shape of my hand. It's my "go to" hammer, my first choice when I need to pound something. Every now and then, when I lay my favorite hammer down and can't remember where, I use one of the others. I'm sure it's my imagination, but I never feel quite as comfortable with those hammers as I do with my favorite.

> People in love with their tools . . . are frequently biased and limited in their approach to problem solving.

I'm not the exception. People have a tendency to fall in love with tools. Those "tools" may be a favorite hammer, a preferred piece of software, or a long-established way of doing things. We return to them time and again, preferring their familiarity to the uncertainty of "things different." Our love affair with our tools often skews how we define a problem. Psychologist Abraham Maslow once said, "If the only tool you have is a hammer, you treat everything like a nail."

People in love with their tools—ideas, traditions, equipment—are frequently biased and limited in their approach to problem solving. These people are not only opposed to out-of-the-box thinking, they would prefer, if at all possible, to take their favorite hammer and nail the box shut! Our tools serve us well, until we become so comfortable with them that we are no longer able to consider other options and approaches. Tools then become our masters, dictating courses of action that often lead us away from the solutions we seek. This was the state of the heavier-than-air flying problem at the dawn of the twentieth century. Solving the problem would require those who did so to look for solutions outside their comfort zones. This was a barrier most could not penetrate.

Theories

Historian J. H. Elliott has written extensively on the demise of Imperial Spain. Detailing reasons for the empire's fall, Elliott wrote, "They could not bring themselves at the moment of crisis to surrender their memories and alter the antique patterns of their lives." In other words, their prejudices robbed them of the ability to "flex" with the times. The same problem was retarding progress on the heavier-than-air flying problem. Many great and learned men were unable to "surrender their memories" and consider alternative options. There was no shortage of ideas and approaches to the problem at the end of the nineteenth century. There were four theories, however, that dominated.

Theory 1: Bird's Rule

Otto Lilienthal, the German engineer and gliding expert, was convinced that the key to solving the problem of manned flight was to emulate the action of birds. Lilienthal wrote an important book in 1899 called *Birdflight as the Basis for Aviation*. Although his approach would prove unsuccessful, Lilienthal was a methodical researcher who captured and recorded important data on lift and drag, data that later would be used by the Wright brothers. Not surprisingly, Lilienthal's designs bore a strong resemblance to bird wings. He was convinced that birds propelled themselves by the action of wing tips, and he sought to duplicate this motion himself. Even when Lilienthal began looking at motors as a way of powering his gliders, his concept was to power movable wing tips, not propellers. It was a personal prejudice with which he was never able to part.

Theory 2: Power Rules

Sir Hiram Maxim was obsessed with the belief that manned flight depended on the creation of an engine powerful enough to propel the craft into the air. Unable to focus on anything but this issue, he gave no consideration whatsoever to a means of controlling his machine once it was in the air. He believed that a flying machine with sufficient power could be flown in a straight line without difficulty. That accomplished, "other problems" (e.g., control and balance) could then be addressed. Once a proper motor was developed, Maxim believed, the problem of heavier-than-air manned flight would be solved.

Theory 3: Speed Rules

As a trained civil engineer, Samuel Langley took a more scientific approach to the problem, conducting experiments with models. The incorrect conclusion Langley arrived at, one that would become known as Langley's Law, was that the faster the speed, the less force was required to sustain flight. As a result, Langley's emphasis was on increasing power while reducing weight.

Although Langley had earlier noted the importance of control and balance in flight, he put these critical issues aside and focused efforts on his prejudices. When Lilienthal heard of Langley's approach, he warned him against making his machines so light they would not withstand the forces of nature. Langley ignored the warnings. Langley's first attempt to fly his *Great Aerodrome* in October 1903 ended when it collapsed on takeoff due to structural weakness. His second attempt two months later failed for the same reason. Langley's bias kept him from even considering another approach.

Theory 4: Automatic Stability

When the Wright brothers first wrote Octave Chanute and told him of their plans to fly at Kitty Hawk, the Chicago engineer and aviation pioneer was greatly alarmed. Chanute firmly believed that the key to heavier-than-air manned flight was to build automatic stability into the structure; any other approach would invite disaster. Chanute agreed with the Wright brothers that Lilienthal's method of controlling his gliders by swinging his body to counterbalance movement was impractical. Instead of considering ways of managing the inherent instability of the craft by creating the means of controlling it, Chanute focused his attention on developing automatic systems, a task at which he never succeeded.

Chanute's structured career as a civil engineer had dulled his ability to consider options outside his personal experience. He had spent virtually his entire life building structures (e.g., bridges and railroads) that emphasized strength and stability, not to mention the safety of the public. As a result, he was unable to approach the problem of heavier-than-air manned flight without these being primary considerations. Chanute was unable to overcome the burden of his personal biases. Although they greatly valued Chanute's friendship and counsel, the Wright brothers would never get over his seeming inability to consider new approaches to the problem of flight.

> The prejudices of some experimenters became stumbling blocks in the way of grasping the truth.

The Wright Approach

As bicycle builders, the Wright brothers were not put off by inherent instability. They felt that automatic controls were unachievable, and even undesirable, at that point in time. Automatic controls not only would be unreliable, but would give the operator a false sense of security. By being flexible enough to consider inherent instability as a benefit, the Wright brothers were able to create a system of control that could be learned in much the same way one learned to balance and control a bicycle. From the beginning, balance and control, not power, propulsion, or automatic stability, was the focus of the Wrights.

The inability of Lilienthal, Langley, and Chanute, as well as a score of others, to "surrender their memories" may have kept one of them from solving the problem of heavier-than-air powered flight. Their prejudices became stumbling blocks in the way of grasping the truth. Although the Wright brothers appreciated structure and method as much as anyone, they were unfettered by such prejudices. The Wright brothers' imaginations were free to explore all possibilities. It was the difference between success and failure.

Creative Thinking

Creativity over the years has been defined in many ways. One of the best (and simplest) definitions I've encountered is this: Creativity is the ability to have new thoughts. Mike Vance, the creativity expert who fathered "out of the box" thinking, offers another definition: "Creativity is the making of the new and the rearranging of the old in a new way." I like Vance's definition because it recognizes both the birthing and nurturing elements of the creative process. Invention-extension—that is, advancing existing ideas and knowledge by providing additional interpretation or application—is just as important (perhaps more so) as the ability to come up with original concepts.

Many people now honored for their "making of the new" actually deserve to be applauded for "rearranging the old." Henry Ford was not the first American to invent the gasoline-powered automobile. John Lambert did that in 1891. Ford, however, created the assembly line and popularized the gas-powered car. Samuel Morse, often noted as the father of the telegraph, successfully exploited Joseph Henry's invention. Morse demonstrated "invention-extension" by perfecting the telegraph wires and creating Morse code. Alexander Graham Bell was trying to improve on Morse's work by creating a harmonic telegraph. He ended up inventing the telephone.

I have a picture in my office of the drawing Thomas Edison submitted with his patent request for a phonograph. The picture is not that attractive, but I display it because it reminds me of an important lesson.

Many companies, in their effort to encourage "out of the box" thinking, make the mistake of defining the box in all-negative fashion.

Edison's invention was the first in its field, a dramatic achievement. Yet every component used to make it had existed for decades. Edison simply took the old and rearranged it in a new way. Henry Ford, Robert Fulton, Samuel Morse—all took existing knowledge and pushed it forward, creating breakthrough products in the process. Although the Wright brothers were the original authors of the solution to flight, the basic raw materials they used to solve the key problem of control and balance had been around for a hundred years.

Teach Me How to Think, Not What to Think

The creative process involves seamlessly slipping in and out of structure, and it is essential to effective problem solving. Most of the companies I know have, in some form or fashion, tried to bring the "think outside the box" mind-set into their culture. They encourage employees to break free of the cords (i.e., traditions) that bind them and chart new territory. Companies urging employees to think outside the box without understanding the purpose of the box, however, run the risk of getting their ideas off the ground with no practical way of landing them.

Many companies make the mistake of defining the box in all-negative fashion. Employees begin to see the box as some kind of thinking "evil." During problem-solving workshops, I often ask participants for their definition of the box. Their answers reveal a lot about their company cultures. One person offered the opinion that the box was what you carried all those policies and procedures around in. Participants often describe the box as:

- The status quo (i.e., the pressure on all sides to keep things the way they are)

- Root-bound (i.e., having no room to grow and no chance of being transplanted)

- Tradition (i.e., long ago someone decided . . .)

- Groupthink (i.e., if you need an idea, we'll tell you what it is)

- Rigid thinking (i.e., an unbending attitude)

- A pen (i.e., an enclosure)

- A pine box (i.e., where creativity goes to die)

Many individuals view the box as a sort of repository for stale, conformed thought, a creativity-binding enclosure that must be escaped at all costs. If you fail to properly define the box, then encouraging people to leave it can lead to what I call "problematic creativity." Here's an example: A component maker in the electronics industry needs a product feature that will set it apart from competitors. Encouraging its engineers to go "outside the box" for new ideas, it is able to come up with a truly unique product concept. The feature is so unique, however, that potential buyers cannot find a second source for it. Without a back-up supplier (an industry no-no), buyers cannot order the part. Problematic creativity, creativity burdened with compromising factors, keeps the new product from getting off the ground.

The Case for the Box

The box takes a beating in the creative process. Nothing of value, it would seem, ever occurs there. In reality, nothing of value can occur *without* the box. If creativity represents the flexible mind at work, the box represents the structure needed to give that creativity purposeful form. Earlier I defined this marriage of flexibility and rigidity as mind-warping. Let me revisit my earlier definition of the term: Mind-warping is a problem-solving principle that provides the mental flexibility to consider nonstandard options without discarding the benefits of structure (known truths).

Ironically, those who see the "box" as a safety net that keeps us from considering nonstandard possibilities run the risk of making "out of the box" thinking a comfort zone as well, one that frees the individual from the responsibility of having to bring ideas to a constructive conclusion. "True freedom," Erich Fromm notes, "is not the absence of structure, but rather a clear structure that enables people to work within established boundaries in an autonomous and creative way." And that includes the freedom of slipping in and out of that structure.

Mind-Warping, The Wright Way

Few people realize that the Wright brothers were publishers and printers before they were bicycle builders or aviation pioneers. Orville was the first to express an interest in printing, spending two summers as an apprentice at a printing company. Then, in the spring of 1888, he decided to build his own press. The design was a good one, but Orville struggled in bringing it together at the end, so he welcomed Wilbur's offer to help. Although many of the suggestions Wilbur made for the press defied mechanical logic (i.e., "we've never done it that way before"), their homemade printing press functioned flawlessly.

Later, when the representative of a Chicago printing company stopped by to look at the press (after word of its effectiveness had spread), he scratched his head in wonder. "Well, it works," he said, "but I certainly don't see how." That the Wright brothers knew how to go "out of bounds" for solutions would be, in the days to come, one of the key factors in their ability to solve complex and challenging problems, including heavier-than-air flight.

Learning to Soar

In the 1980s, the American Management Association published a study stating that the best managers in the future would be those with a "high tolerance for ambiguity." The ability to mind-warp (i.e., slip effortlessly between the abstract and the concrete) may well be the survival skill of the future. Here are a few tips to help make the transition. Most apply to organizations as well as individuals:

- *Engage perplexities.* There is a tendency for many of us to step around those things we do not immediately comprehend. Instead of regarding periods of uncertainty and puzzlement as opportunities to learn and grow, we see them as potential entanglements with negative outcomes. It takes mental and emotional commitment to get comfortable with the unknown while seeking to know it. Make it a point to explore and learn about something you do not presently understand.

- *Energize and empower curiosity.* Organizations staffed with individuals who possess a strong desire to explore, investigate, and learn will have a significant competitive advantage in the future. Curiosity fuels the creative process, which in turn fills the new idea (e.g., product, process, or strategy) pipeline. Energize curiosity by reinforcing its value in the problem-solving process. Ask staff members to identify things that intrigue them, then encourage them by rewarding, reinforcing, and respecting their efforts to pursue those interests, even if there is no immediate benefit to the organization. Remember, without curiosity, there can be no growth.

- *Develop whole-world vision.* The ability to explore an opportunity without being encumbered by traditional organizational blinders is crucial. Encourage your team to look at problems in something more than a local (i.e., individual, departmental, or company) sense. Encourage them to expand their vision, to explore possibilities that might be seen only by taking a larger view. You can encourage this practice in meetings by exploring the consequences of a decision on both a macro and a micro level.

- *Get comfortable with contradiction.* Contradictions are ideas and approaches that seem to defy common sense, and they are often the starting point in the process of invention-extension. Contradiction can stimulate new ideas and concepts, much as a grain of sand in an oyster can stimulate the creation of a priceless gem. A subset of uncertainty, contradiction can be a key source of energy in powering creative and productive thinking. To get comfortable with contradiction, encourage employees to defend positions and ideas that run contrary to those presently held.

- *Increase risk-taking propensity.* Steering clear of hazardous situations is a part of the culture of many organizations. Yet risks are often opportunities in disguise. Individuals and organizations that implement risk-aversion strategies without also considering risk-exploiting ones rob themselves of opportunities for significant growth. Foolish risks should be avoided, but in risking nothing, organizations may end up risking it all. The Wright brothers understood this and, though cautious by nature, were willing to risk life and fortune on an admittedly risky idea.

- *Get comfortable with instability.* "If man will begin with certainties," Francis Bacon once wrote, "he shall end in doubts." The inherent instability (i.e., ambiguity) we face must be welcomed, embraced, and even entertained if breakthrough thinking is to occur. The most effective organizations in the future will be the ones with a high tolerance for rapid change and ambiguity. These companies will routinely upset the status quo by soliciting nontraditional approaches and ideas from their teams.

The Wright Home at 7 Hawthorn Street in Dayton

During the slow months, Wilbur and Orville had busied themselves with a variety of projects. They remodeled their home on Hawthorn Street, adding a wraparound porch and shutters to improve its appearance. [Chapter 7]

The Wright brothers' meticulous attention to detail is evident in the uniformity of the porch columns, hand-turned by the brothers on a neighbor's lathe. Orville was born in this house in 1871, and Wilbur died here in 1912. Henry Ford purchased the house in 1938 and moved it to his Greenfield Village Museum in Dearborn, Michigan.

Wilbur at Work at the Wright Cycle Company, 1897

New tools began to find their way into the Williams Street shop: a turret lathe, drill press, tube cutting equipment. They attached the tools to an overhead shaft with pulleys, then designed and built a small illuminating gas-powered engine to drive them. Their bicycles were known for their craftsmanship and attention to detail. [Chapter 4]

As they manufactured and repaired bicycles, the Wright brothers were acquiring the mental and physical skills they would later use to construct their flying machine. Many features used to construct their bicycles would be incorporated into the design of their 1903 *Wright Flyer.*

Wilbur Executes a Right Hand Turn

Wilbur was working in his bicycle shop one day when a customer came in to purchase an inner tube. While talking with the customer, Wilbur began fiddling with the cardboard box the tube had come in. As he twisted it in his hands, he noticed how the top and bottom of the box behaved when he rotated it. In his mind, he could picture the same effect on the double-deck wings of a flying machine. [Chapter 5]

The concept that Wilbur discovered (wing-warping), using the problem solving principle of inveterate tinkering, would later evolve into a method for making controlled turns. The wing-warping feature is evident in the picture above, where the twist in the wings can be easily seen.

Wilbur Fails at First Attempt to Fly

While the little 12hp engine was warming up, Wilbur and Orville drew aside from the others. One of the brothers, probably Wilbur, reached into his pocket, pulled out a coin, and flipped it into the air. Wilbur won the toss and, after shaking hands with Orville, slid into place on the lower wing of the Wright Flyer. [Chapter 9]

Wilbur won the coin toss, but failed in his first attempt at powered and controlled flight. Still learning to control the machine, Wilbur turned the forward elevator up too soon, forcing the flyer into a stall. After the attempt, Wilbur remained in place on the damaged *Flyer,* mentally critiquing his performance

History's First Powered and Controlled Flight

In aviation circles, the first-flight photograph of Orville Wright is referred to simply as "The Shot." Regarded by many as the most famous photograph in aviation history (it's certainly the most reproduced), the picture captures the moment the Wright Flyer *lifts off its starting track.* [Chapter 8]

Around 10:35 A.M. on December 17, 1903, Orville Wright achieved the first powered and controlled flight in a heavier-than-air machine. The flight lasted twelve seconds and covered a distance of 120 feet. Later, Wilbur would record a flight lasting 59 seconds and covering 852 feet, the best of the day.

Replica of the Wright Brothers' 1901 Wind Tunnel

If December 17, 1903, qualifies as the most important date in aviation history, November 22, 1901, would have to be the second. That was the day the Wright brothers completed work on their new wind tunnel and began making the measurements and calculations that would unravel the mystery of flight. [Chapter 8]

After a discouraging season of test glides in 1901, the Wright brothers suspected the data contained in Lilienthal's lift and drag tables might be in error. To confirm their suspicions, they constructed an ingenious wind tunnel to test small balances modeling wing shapes. Their methodical and meticulous efforts yielded data that is accurate a hundred years later.

History's First Fatality in a Powered Airplane

In 1908, while trying to qualify his flyer for the military, Orville took Lieutenant Thomas Selfridge up with him as passenger. While aloft, the flyer broke a propeller. The machine spun out of control and crashed to the ground in seconds. [Chapter 1]

In the fall of 1908, Orville was conducting test flights at Fort Myers to qualify their flyer for military purchase. The military required that the machine be able to carry a passenger. In the crash, Orville suffered injuries that would cause him pain the rest of his life. Selfridge became the first fatality in a powered airplane crash.

Wilbur and Orville on the Back Porch at Hawthorn Street

Whereas Wilbur wore his clothes, Orville displayed them. . . . [Here] Wilbur, wearing a somewhat rumpled suit, is slouched against the wall. Orville on the other hand, is sitting ramrod straight, with hands folded over knees. A sharp crease is evident in his trousers, which are pulled up to reveal a natty pair of argyle socks. [Introduction]

By June 1909, Wilbur and Orville Wright were two of the most famous men in the world. In this photo, the personality styles of the two men are apparent. Different in so many respects, it was what they shared in common that made their partnership a success: a passionate belief that man could fly.

→ *Let fantasies guide you.* Sometimes it's useful to temporarily suspend the rules and guidelines that govern day-to-day thinking and action. Don't discard an idea or thought just because it seems silly or falls short of someone's idea of what "makes sense."

→ *Look for new ideas in related activities.* While observing the wing tips of birds in flight, the Wright brothers discovered a new idea for making controlled turns with their glider. Activities that run parallel to our own can often be sources of new approaches or breakthrough ideas. Encourage team members to engage in related activities to keep ideas from being limited to the confines of daily routines.

Learning to flex one's brain, individually or collectively, as a corporation, may take some getting used to, especially if you've functioned, as most of us have, in a highly structured environment. The rewards for making the effort, however, can be extraordinary.

One Last Thought

Long before the life-altering events of September 11, business was dealing with the unnerving effects of an unstable and erratic world. Economic turbulence, market uncertainty, and quixotic customer behavior—all ensured that change was no longer episodic, but chronic, in our lives. Although many of us are still hoping for a return to normal, the reality is that a "new normal" has emerged in the form of inherent instability. For many, it is a world filled with obstacles to be avoided. For others, it's a world filled with nuggets of opportunity, but requiring new skills to mine them. At or near the top of the skills list should be mind-warping, the ability to move seamlessly between the abstract and the concrete—or, put another way, to be logical while rationally considering the illogical.

The reality is that a "new normal" has emerged in the form of inherent instability.

When you first learned to ride a bicycle, you probably received some assistance in managing its inherent instability. This came in the form of a steadying hand of a parent, or a set of training wheels. It was assumed, however, that these were temporary aides that would be removed once the skill was mastered. In business today, there are some people—even in high positions of authority—who are still looking for a steadying hand to guide them through the instability of their environment. Their "training wheels" usually come in the form of strict adherence to tradition, procedure, and past experience. As new expressions of instability continue to present themselves, these individuals are anxious to return to the "good old days" instead of looking for new possibilities.

Wilbur and Orville Wright, different in so many ways, were both crisp, logical thinkers. Wilbur especially hated guesswork and would exhaust all possibilities in searching for answers. While both of them were methodical and meticulous in their approach (see Chapter 8), they still had the capacity to consider options outside their frame of reference. Had the Wright brothers been able to gain "new truth" from any other flying-machine experimenters, they most surely would have, preferring to benefit from others' experience. Despite their meticulousness, the brothers were more than able to relax the rigidity of known structure.

Years ago Abraham Maslow began citing the need for a new flexibility. "Life is moving far more rapidly," he noted, "than ever before. We need a different kind of human being," he continued, "able to live in a world that changes perpetually, who has been educated to be comfortable with change." Three decades later, our world has grown more complex than Maslow could have ever dreamed. The solution, as Wilbur and Orville discovered, may well be the ability to coexist with that instability. Instead of trying to eliminate it, learn to control it and make it work for you.

CHAPTER SEVEN

RELENTLESS PREPARATION

THE PRINCIPLE OF FOREVER LEARNING

Learners will inherit the future.
Eric Hoffer (1902–1983), philosopher

RELENTLESS PREPARATION is a problem-solving principle that says that "forever learning"—learning as a lifelong passion—is essential to generating the information needed to solve problems. Forever learning draws a dotted line between the need to solve problems and the reservoir of ideas we possess to do so. Forever learning, a vital part of preparation, is the process of keeping that reservoir full.

*   *   *

When Michelangelo, as a young man of thirteen, applied for an art apprenticeship in his native Florence, he was asked curtly, "Can you draw?" "I have the capacity to learn," he replied. His answer became the theme of his life. Irving Stone, in his biographical novel *The Agony and the Ecstasy*, says Michelangelo "absorbed instruction like a dehydrated sponge thrown into the Arno River." His appetite for knowledge, powered by an insatiable curiosity, caused him to pursue learning opportunities with remarkable intensity. When asked at the age of eighty-four to summarize his life's philosophy, Michelangelo replied in his native tongue, *"Ancora imparo"* (and still I learn). Michelangelo's journey from apprentice at thirteen to godlike acclaim at eighty-nine was powered each step by his capacity to learn, and his commitment to do so all the days of his life.

Wanted: A Defining Purpose

Wilbur was restless during the winter of 1898. After peaking the previous year, his bicycle business had steadily declined as the market became saturated. It wasn't the drop in sales that most concerned him, however. During the slow months, he and Orville had busied themselves with a variety of projects. They remodeled their home on Hawthorn Street, adding a wraparound porch and shutters to improve its appearance. Inside, entire walls were moved to create more efficient living space. The craftsmanship, as usual, was excellent. But Wilbur knew he was using "busyness" to keep from confronting a growing concern. At age thirty-five, he realized his small business ventures would never satisfy a growing desire to do something significant.

Wilbur's concerns about his future may have been aroused by concerns for one of his nephews. Herbert, the son of Reuchlin and Lulu Wright, was a lackluster youth who seemed without ambition and drive. During a visit to Dayton, the boy's mother confided to the Wright family that Herbert was a disappointment. She and Reuchlin had decided to skip further education for the boy, opting instead to place him in a "business situation" as soon as possible. Concerned that Herbert was being pushed in a direction for which he had no calling, Wilbur later wrote Lulu:

> I entirely agree that the boys of the Wright family are all lacking in determination and push. None of us has as yet made particular use of the talent in which he excels other men, that is why our success has been moderate.

It was a key statement for Wilbur. Moderate success, more than anything, was the source of his discontent. His nephew's shortcomings had
forced him to confront his own shortcomings and the gnawing absence of
a defining purpose. The challenge he sought, that defining purpose, was
about to present itself. It would tax his abilities as nothing had before or
would ever do again. It would give more meaning and purpose to his life
than he had ever imagined. It would not, however, catch him unprepared.

Preparing for Opportunity

Many of those writing about the Wright brothers like to point out the fact
that they were high school dropouts. Although it makes for an interesting story, it's a bit misleading. Wilbur, an excellent scholar, completed the
requirements for graduation in Richmond, Indiana. During his senior
year he carried an aggressive load of classes that included Greek, Latin,
geometry, natural philosophy, and composition, scoring high marks in
each subject. A voracious reader, he supplemented this schoolwork with
unassigned studies at home. Shortly before commencement, Bishop
Wright moved his family to Dayton. Wilbur, who believed that the knowledge gained from education was more important than a piece of paper,
didn't feel a diploma was worth a fifty-mile return journey to attend the
commencement ceremony. By failing to attend commencement, Wilbur
technically never graduated. Orville's journey was more eclectic.

By all accounts, Orville was a handful as a child. His father described
him as "excitable," others as inquisitive and impulsive. He was a cheerful little guy who had a hard time sticking with the program. Enrolled
at the age of five in kindergarten, Orville went to class for four days
before deciding it wasn't for him. Every morning he would leave the
house as if headed to school. Instead of going to class, however, he
sneaked over to the house of Ed Sine, a neighborhood friend, where he
and the Sine boy spent the day tinkering with an old sewing machine
and whatever other objects they could find to "inspect." Taking things
apart to see how they worked would remain a lifelong passion of
Orville's. Keeping a watchful eye on the clock, Orville would leave his
friend's house just in time to arrive home at the after-school hour
expected. His deception lasted a month, until his mother, wondering

how he was progressing, dropped by his school to see his teacher. Home schooling was immediately implemented.

Although inquisitive, Orville did not possess Wilbur's scholarly approach to his studies. When he was expelled from school late in his sixth-grade year for playing a prank (he loved practical jokes), he decided to take the rest of the year off. It was a fact he neglected to mention at home. It wasn't until his parents tried to enroll Orville in the seventh grade after moving to Dayton that they discovered what he had done. Despite his occasional absences, Orville did well in school, especially on topics that interested him. One story gives a peek into his academic prowess, while offering a glimpse of the personality that would one day make him a valued partner to Wilbur.

Orville was merely demonstrating a problem-solving strategy he would use often in the future: Always look for the second "right answer."

In the ninth grade, Orville was asked to explain a geometry problem on the blackboard. When he finished, his teacher gave him credit for arriving at the correct answer, but chastised him for not following the procedure in the textbook. Orville explained that he had been reading *Wentworth's Geometry,* an unassigned textbook, on the side and preferred the approach to the problem presented in that book. It may have been the first time Orville had discarded one approach in favor of another, but it would not be the last. Orville was merely demonstrating a problem-solving strategy he would use often in the future: Always look for the second "right answer."

Orville was a good student (especially in mathematics), but commerce had won his heart. When he was ten, he was building and selling kites to friends. That enterprise was later followed by a junk-dealing business, a chewing-gum-making scheme, and a bone-collecting (for resale to a fertilizer company) operation. He had tasted the excitement of small business and was hooked. An interest in printing led to the acquisition of a small printing press. He and Wilbur later collaborated on building a larger press, then went into business together for the first time, publishing a small newspaper called *The West Side News.* In *Grand Eccentrics,* Mark Bernstein writes of Orville, "*The News* turned printing from a hobby into a business, thus providing the excuse he needed for skipping out of his senior year." Orville dropped out of school not running from *but to* something.

Home Schooling

In reading about the Wright brothers' school years, you might get the impression that education in the Wright household was not a priority. Nothing could be further from the truth. Milton Wright, a bishop in the United Brethren Church, had strongly held beliefs regarding education that did not always line up with those of public school. Although he endorsed formal education, he believed that learning opportunities were all around. He had a penchant for encouraging his children to skip school now and then to explore something that had captured their interest. This did not sit well with teachers and school administrators.

Far from neglecting his children's education, the Bishop was expanding it. Eric Hoffer, the longshoreman turned philosopher, said the central task of education was to "implant a will and facility for learning." The goal of education is to not produce "learned" but "learning" people. Milton Wright believed that education was essential, but that the emphasis should be placed on teaching his offspring how to learn, not just what to learn. The Bishop knew the value of knowledge, and he made sure his children—including daughter Katharine—were frequently exposed to learning opportunities.

What Did You Bring Me, Daddy?

The elder Wright, who traveled extensively in his work as a bishop, would often return with an educational toy or interesting artifact (e,g., a seashell, bottle of sand, etc.) for his children. One such toy, a rubber band–powered helicopter, was later credited by Orville as the beginning of their interest in aviation. Milton Wright's effort to educate his children, however, was not limited to toys and interesting artifacts.

If there was one passion in the Wright family that rose over all others, it was their love of books. Sunday in the Wright household was reserved for reading and letter writing. Games such as card playing were discouraged, not because they were sinful, but because they were a waste of time. Wilbur, due to a prolonged illness, had become the more prolific reader of the group, but Orville and Katharine were not far behind. All three Wright siblings found ample material in the two well-stocked libraries maintained by their father. Milton Wright had a remarkable collection of books by the standards of the day, and they were well used.

The library on the first floor of the Wright home was easily the favorite. Fred Howard describes its contents in his Wright brother biography, *Wilbur and Orville:*

> The downstairs library, with its fashionable sets of Irving, Hawthorne, *The Spectator,* Scott, and Gibbons, was more eclectic. It included multivolume histories of England and France, natural history books, Grimm, Andersen, Plutarch's *Lives,* and two sets of encyclopedias.

Years later, Wilbur would be widely acclaimed in France and England for his knowledge of these countries' history and culture, which could be directly traced to the books pulled off the shelves in his home. It's interesting to note that Wilbur's favorite reading was Plutarch's *Lives,* from which he gained a great appreciation for strategy and disciplined thinking. Orville, on the other hand, had an insatiable appetite for the scientific articles in the *Chambers* and *Britannica* encyclopedias at his disposal.

The upstairs library, maintained by the Bishop for his work, was a more serious collection. In addition to books on religion and philosophy, Milton Wright had books by noted atheists Charles Darwin and Robert Ingersoll. The father made no attempt to direct or control the reading of his children. Every book—including those by Darwin and Ingersoll—was available to any family member interested in reading it. Bishop Wright was more concerned that his children become critical thinkers. He wanted his children's inquisitiveness to take them wherever it led. It would eventually lead them, according to aviation historian Sir Charles Gibbs-Smith, to an article in the September 1894 issue of *McClure's Magazine.*

Fanning the Embers

Wilbur and Orville's fascination with flight, dormant since childhood, was roused by an article in *McClure's* on German engineer Otto Lilienthal, who was conducting glider experiments in the Rhinow Hills outside Berlin. The brothers were captivated, as were people all over the world, by newspaper and magazine photographs of the intrepid aviator soaring in his glider. That interest, as usual, drove the brothers into books, magazines, and other periodicals in pursuit of anything they could learn about Lilienthal and manned flight. Although the brothers would read everything they could find on aviation over the next two years, it would not be enough to satisfy their considerable interest in the problem of heavier-than-air flight.

> The Wright brothers did what their father had taught them to do since their youth: They engaged their perplexities.

In August 1896, while Orville was recovering from a serious bout of typhoid fever, Wilbur read a news story reporting Lilienthal's death in a gliding accident. According to the article, Lilienthal's glider had been upset by a gust of wind. Swinging his legs in a desperate attempt to regain control of the vehicle, he had plunged some fifty feet to the ground. He lingered in a Berlin hospital for two days after his accident before succumbing to his injuries. His last words were, "Sacrifices must be made." Lilienthal's death, while tragic, did not dampen the interest of the Wright brothers. If anything, it heightened it. Wilbur later wrote:

> My own active interest in aeronautical problems dates back to the death of Lilienthal in 1896. The brief notice of his death which appeared in the telegraphic news at that time aroused a passive interest which had existed from my childhood and led me to take down from the shelves of our home library a book on *Animal Mechanism,* by Professor [Etienne Jules] Marey, which I had already read several times. From this I was led to read more modern works, and as my brother soon became equally interested with myself we soon passed from the reading to the thinking, and finally to the working stage.

The brothers not only wanted to know more about Lilienthal's experiments, but what others had accomplished in the field as well. The Wright family passion for learning was clearly revealed in Wilbur and Orville at this time, ignited by Lilienthal's misfortune and the unanswered questions it left behind. The Wright brothers, energized by the vagaries of the problem, did what their father had taught them to do since their youth: They engaged their perplexities. They started, of course, by learning everything they could about the problem.

The Heart of the Matter

A reporter, looking for a special insight into how the Wright brothers had solved the problem of flight, was given a clue by Bishop Wright. "For several years," he replied, "they (Wilbur and Orville) read up on aeronautics as a physician would read his books." The parallel the Bishop was trying to draw was that a physician reads with great diligence, knowing that someone's life may depend on the knowledge he acquires. Wilbur and Orville pursued knowledge in a similar fashion, knowing that their lives may be put at risk as well.

Whenever the Wright brothers had an interest in something, they immediately sought more information on the subject, going to other sources, if necessary, when the resources in their home library were not enough. It was their one uncompromising habit in solving problems. Consider the following:

- At the age of twelve, Orville becomes interested in woodcutting after reading an article in *Century Magazine.* He immediately goes to the library to read everything he can about the subject, and he later applies this knowledge to develop his own woodcuts.

- Exhausting home and public library resources on aviation, Wilbur writes to the Smithsonian Institution to request recommendations and materials. He purchases every book recommended by the Smithsonian, rereading the books many times. The original books, which are on display at Wright State University, have pencil notes in the margins.

- When the brothers begin work on the propellers for their 1903 *Wright Flyer,* their first step is to visit the public library and find everything they can on marine technology (propellers were already in use on power ships).

"The time expended in preliminary study of books was not misspent," Orville told biographer Fred Kelly, "for they gave us a good general understanding of the subject, and enabled us at the outset to avoid effort in many directions in which results would have been hopeless."

Disciplined and methodical thinkers, Wilbur and Orville had a low tolerance for guesswork. If information on the subject was already available, that was the starting point. Once the information was consumed, discussions between the brothers would begin with the following questions:

- What is the objective (i.e., the problem to be solved)?

- What has already been done?

- What can we learn from previous efforts, both successes and failures?

- Can the problem be reduced to smaller subsets?

- Is information available on those subsets?

- What information will we need to solve this problem?

- What skills will be required to solve this problem?

- What resources (e.g., materials, equipment, etc.) will be needed to solve this problem?

- What obstacles will need to be overcome to solve this problem?

For the Wright brothers, who systemized everything, it was an orderly process powered at all times by their commitment to continually learn and grow. They solved the problem of heavier-than-air flight, as much as anything, by thoroughly studying it. It was something others had neglected to do.

When Wilbur and Orville's interest in manned flight was reignited in 1896, it was quite natural for them to do what they had learned to do from their earliest days: Read all about it. Books on the subject of flight were scarce, however. In their book *Twelve Seconds to the Moon*, Rosamond Young and Catharine Fitzgerald report that Orville was more than a bit frustrated with the Dayton Public Library's lack of books on the subject of manned flight. When he asked the librarian why there were no books on aeronautics, he was told that "scientists held the idea in great discredit and it was therefore not a subject on which libraries spend money."

The brothers were not deterred. They continued their research by rereading articles they had previously uncovered in magazines and wearing out their encyclopedia. They read everything they could get their hands on for *three years*. It wasn't enough, however, to satisfy a rapidly increasing appetite. When Wilbur took pen in hand and wrote to the Smithsonian Institution on May 30, 1899, to request information on aeronautics, he created what was arguably the most important letter the Smithsonian has ever received. Wilbur took pains to let the Smithsonian know that he was genuinely interested in the topic as an "enthusiast, not a crank." He wrote the Smithsonian that he wanted to avail himself of all that was already known, with an eye toward adding "his mite" to the solution.

The letter was received by the Smithsonian on June 2, and responded to by Richard Rathbun, Samuel Langley's personal assistant. Rathbun instructed his clerk to send Wilbur several articles that had appeared in the *Smithsonian Annual Report* on flight. The collection included excerpts from Louis-Pierre Mouillard's "Empire of the Air;" Langley's "The Story of Experiments in Mechanical Flight"; Otto Lilienthal's "The Problem of Flying and Practical Experiments in Soaring"; and E. C. Huffaker's "On Soaring Flight." In a separate note, Rathbun recommended three books: *Progress in Flying Machines,* by Octave Chanute; *Experiments in Aerodynamics,* by Langley; and *The Aeronautical Annual,* by James Howard Means. The books were immediately ordered by Wilbur.

When the books and materials from the Smithsonian arrived, the brothers were ecstatic. In *Wilbur and Orville: A Biography of the Wright Brothers,* Fred Howard describes the reading material as "a rich feast for two bicycle mechanics whose diet until then had been restricted to books on ornithology, encyclopedia articles on bird flight, and an occasional magazine piece on man's attempt to fly." The brothers often became so absorbed in reading (and debating) that all other thoughts slipped away, including a commitment made to sister Katharine to entertain friends she had brought home from Oberlin College. Their intense focus on the problem at hand would have made both brothers, had either married, a poor choice for a mate.

In *The Wright Brothers,* biographer Fred Kelly tells the story of a friend who once commented to Orville that he and his brother would always be an example of how young men with no special advantages could get ahead. Orville immediately took exception, saying that they did have special advantages. "We were lucky enough," he explained, "to grow up in a home environment where there was always much encouragement to pursue intellectual interests; to investigate whatever aroused curiosity. In a different kind of environment," he continued, "our curiosity might have been nipped long before it could have borne fruit." The success of the Wright brothers was forged in an environment that fanned the flames of potential.

Curiosity Strategy: Nip It!

I can't help but think, when reading Orville's words, how much they apply to the workplace today. Employees fortunate enough to work in an environment where they're encouraged to be inquisitive, to pursue ideas and concepts, are few and far between. Most companies, it seems, are more in the "nip it" business. These companies are frequently characterized by cultures that discourage original or independent thinking. Criticisms are commonplace, with novel thinking something to keep an eye on. Employees are more often schooled in what they shouldn't be doing, rather than encouraged to use their judgment.

Companies obsessed with "hammering down nails" deprive themselves of a critically needed resource: new ideas.

There's a story about a man who was hired to work at Thomas Edison's famous Menlo Park laboratory. Reporting for his first day of work, he asked Edison what the laboratory regulations were. Edison nearly exploded. "There ain't no rules around here," he yelled, "we're trying to accomplish something!" When companies stifle the curiosity of their employees, they run the risk of creating an environment characterized by fear, disapproval, and extreme cautiousness. The result is a demotivated workforce, one in which it is hard to inspire or enthuse people, or get new and original ideas from them.

Constrained Curiosity

An insatiable inquisitiveness acquired in their youth powered the Wright brothers through every step that led to their December 17, 1903, flight. It was essential to the Wright brothers, and it is essential to the success of businesses of every type and category today. Regrettably, it appears to be one of the least valued commodities in business. A quick survey of organizations reveals that a desire to know *why* is often subjugated to a philosophy that says to "get with the program." Constrained curiosity is a policy destined to come up short, to stall at the end of the runway.

Examples of companies dampening the curiosity of employees abound. Several years ago I was asked by a company to conduct a survey of past and present employees. I found it difficult to get much of value from present employees, but the people who had left were a veritable gold mine of information. Most indicated they liked working for my client because as a company, it had a great reputation. Almost everyone, however, cited intolerance toward creativity as the primary reason they left. As one former employee expressed it, "They're obsessed with hammering down nails over there." Companies obsessed with "hammering down nails" deprive themselves of a critically needed resource: new ideas.

Understanding some of the ways that companies constrain curiosity is a good starting point for creating systems that can reverse that tendency. Some typical curiosity constrainers are:

➡ Emphasis on tasks instead of outcomes

➡ Long-standing habits or customs

➡ Poor leadership (curiosity not valued)

➡ Obsession with current "tools"

➡ Obsession with risk management

➤ High levels of employee anxiety and fear

➤ Criticism assessed without explanation

➤ Disinterested and disengaged management

In the previously cited example, employees didn't leave the company because of monetary inequities. Many had, in fact, moved on to lower-paying jobs. They left because their desire to grow had been stunted.

Relentless Preparation

Relentless preparation, the principle of forever learning, means that in every problem-solving scenario, information is needed to understand and define the problem. This was a critical first step with the Wright brothers. As you read through studies on the brothers' approach to any flight-related problem—equilibrium, lift deficiency, propulsion—the starting point remained the same: expanded reading. You can't adequately define a problem unless you have a thorough understanding of it. One of the key reasons Wilbur and Orville were able to correctly define balance and control as the tyrant issue (see Chapter 4) was that they had first put their hands on everything available in print.

Relentless preparation, however, is more than a reading program. It's the difference between "learning" and being "learned." It is a lifelong mind-set that hungers for information and understanding of the things around us. It is a desire to understand not only that narrow band of knowledge that defines our specific area of expertise, but the broader knowledge that defines our greater lives. As a problem-solving principle, relentless preparation consists of a simple three-point formula: Gather information, ponder, and apply.

Gathering Information

In every book written about the Wright brothers, reference is made to their passion for reading. Both men had an insatiable curiosity about the world around them. That interest was not limited to aviation, either.

Their reading matter ranged from art to literature, medicine to world affairs. Reading gave the brothers a large frame of reference when it came time to consider potential solutions to a problem. As historian Gibbs-Smith notes, their minds were "well stocked."

Gathering information was not limited to reading, however. The Wright brothers acquired additional knowledge through their acute skills of observation. One of the key factors in solving the problem of manned flight was the discovery of a method of warping the wings of their flying machine, enabling it to make turns. The discovery was not inspired by books, but by countless hours of observing birds in flight. Additional information was gathered by paying attention to what others were doing. In studying the flights of Lilienthal, for example, the brothers were able to gather key data that would enable them to define where he had failed.

Pondering

The second ingredient in the principle of relentless preparation is pondering. Once the information has been gathered, it needs to be thoroughly and thoughtfully considered. This is, in my opinion, where the vast majority of us fail. After gathering information, the most common next step is to apply what someone else has done without further thought. Although this often yields a swift solution, it may not yield the best (i.e., most productive, efficient, timely, or profitable) solution. For the Wright brothers, reading without pondering was useless. The data drawn from books was like bread dough that requires kneading and time to rise before it is placed in the oven.

Pondering and thinking are not the same things. Pondering implies a more careful weighing in the mind than thinking. Thinking, in the context I'm using it, has more to do with process and choice. Pondering is more inconclusive. It is withholding judgment until all possibilities have been considered. It is not the search for the right answer; it's the search for the right *answers*. It's the quiet, sober consideration of a problem in an effort to thoroughly understand it. It was in pondering the data they gathered that the Wright brothers were able to uncover the answers they needed.

Application

It wasn't enough for the Wright brothers to gather information and ponder it, they needed to convert the knowledge gained into tangible results. That required application of what they had learned. On the surface, this sounds so obvious as to approach absurdity. But the amount of knowledge that has been acquired in this country and never applied in a practical way is mind-boggling. Consider the last seminar or workshop you attended. Did you commit to making practical use of any part of what was learned as quickly as possible, or was the information just stuffed away in a filing cabinet (real or mental)? Knowledge gained but unapplied remains nothing more than potential.

A Unique Competitive Advantage

For any company to achieve long-term success, it must have a sustainable competitive advantage—that is, some edge or skill that separates it from the crowd. In Marketing 101, I was told there were basically four things that could give a company competitive advantage: a unique product, the lowest price, exceptional customer service, or strong, well-established relationships. Arie de Geus, a planner with Royal Dutch Shell, would say there was only one. "The only truly sustainable competitive advantage in the future," de Geus notes, "may be the ability to learn faster than the competition." Wilbur and Orville would add an "amen" to that statement. Companies that are obsessed with learning, that have a high level of curiosity and inquisitiveness, are typically:

➼ Better prepared to identify threats and opportunities

➼ Better equipped to respond to sudden and rapid change

➼ Better able to generate multiple solutions to a given problem

➼ Known for their enthusiasm, creativity, and responsiveness

➼ Better able to act in the customer's best interest with empowered employees

➼ Better able to keep new-product pipelines full (since there's no shortage of ideas)

For the Wright brothers, Michelangelo's concept of forever learning was a key problem-solving principle. Their ability to make creative connections was in direct proportion to the amount of ideas (knowledge) they had exposed themselves to. Their minds were well stocked, thanks to a lifelong commitment to relentless preparation.

Learning to Soar

Any organization hoping to prosper in the coming decade will have to make relentless preparation (forever learning) an integral part of its competitive strategy. Here are a few tips to make it happen. Some of these suggestions apply to the organization as a whole, some to individuals, and some to both. We'll leave it up to you to figure which is which.

➡ *Prime the pump.* Like those old-fashioned sucker pumps that need to be primed to get the water flowing, it may be necessary to prime the learning habits of individuals. Legend has it that Thomas Watson, the founder of IBM Corp., told his managers he would pay for any seminar or workshop his people wanted to take, even basket weaving! Watson's goal was to place the emphasis on creating a learning habit.

➡ *Make contact with areas of expertise.* Informal surveys conducted in my seminars reveal that a surprisingly large percentage of college graduates fail to make contact with their areas of discipline after graduation. These individuals not only hurt their organizations by failing to update their knowledge, they run the real risk of becoming last year's model in a competitive employment market. Encourage employees at all levels to continue their education—formally or informally. I recommend that, at a minimum, you read a book a month in your area of discipline. As Vince Lombardi once said, "It's what you learn after you've learned it all that counts."

➡ *Encourage inquisitiveness.* In a television interview, astronaut Scott Carpenter was asked what had made him want to go to the moon. "Driving curiosity," he replied. His clip answer doesn't need elaboration. Curiosity makes things happen. It is the driving force behind everything—from the development of new products to improving the processes to make them. Employees encouraged to pull on the thread of curiosity will frequently bring ideas and options to the surface. "Create an institution where people aren't allowed to be curious," Tom Peters says, "and people won't be curious." Or, as I like to express it, any good behavior that goes unacknowledged will eventually disappear. The best way to acknowledge good behavior is by rewarding it in tangible or intangible fashion.

◆ *Don't skim, read.* Reading has fallen on hard times in a culture conditioned by the Internet to surf and skim. Depth of knowledge and understanding, however, come from really getting into a wide range of topics. Creative thinking expert Mike Vance recommends *three hundred* books a year. The fact that his suggestion is greeted with derision is a reflection not on Vance, but on our poor reading capabilities.

◆ *Tailor learning strategies to meet individual styles.* The learning styles of individuals differ just as their personality styles do. Some people are more tactile in their creative efforts than others. They need to be fiddling with things in order to get their creative juices flowing. Others are more conceptual in the process. The key here is to judge the output, not the method. Create or sponsor learning opportunities that take personality and learning styles into consideration. Some people are detail-oriented and like to thoroughly examine an issue. Others are "big picture" people who prefer an overview of a problem. Neither approach is right or wrong. Both, however, need to be considered in preparing a learning strategy.

◆ *Redefine the concept of failure.* It has been often stated, but mistakes are among the greatest and most productive learning experiences people can have. A critical part of the Wright brothers' efforts were devoted to analyzing the failures of others in an effort to learn from them, and not repeat them. In *Visions of a*

Flying Machine, Peter Jakab notes, "Walking through the failures and misunderstandings of others aided the brothers in focusing quickly on the basic problems that needed to be addressed."

➡ *Be an asker of questions.* Irving Stone says Michelangelo depended on the "ever-widening and deepening circles of questions asked and answered" to provide the knowledge he needed to create his masterpieces. The principle of applied inquisitiveness states that problem solving is greatly enhanced by the ability to gather information. And that requires questions to be asked.

➡ *Rediscover the library.* The first step for the Wright brothers, when confronting a problem or opportunity, was to visit their local library. Although the Internet has surpassed libraries as the primary source of information for many people, the library remains a valuable resource. Not only is it a more tactile experience to be able to peruse actual books, catalogs, and archives, it offers the user an excellent "browsing" opportunity. On more than a few occasions, I've discovered something of value when my eye happened to glance over a bookshelf while looking for something else.

➡ *Hire the learning, not the learned.* There are many criteria for hiring new employees, but one that should be at or near the top is the degree to which a candidate accepts personal responsibility (i.e., accountability) for her growth and development. Dr. Samuel Langley was a highly learned man, but he spent two decades in aviation research without gaining a sufficient understanding of the subject. Wilbur and Orville Wright were forever-learning men who solved the problem because they never quit growing.

I was interviewing candidates once for a sales management position. By way of getting things started, I would ask them to introduce themselves. In the course of their comments, candidates would invariably make reference to their experience. One man pointed out that he had ten years of experience in sales. I asked the man if he had read any books recently on sales or management. "No," he replied, "not really." I then asked him what seminars and workshops he had attended lately. "I really don't have time for that," he answered, "I stay pretty busy." I asked him if he had a mentor or was coached in any way by others. "No," he again answered, "I'm a self-taught man." The man, I realized, did not have ten years of experience, but one year ten times over. His lack of a learning program had turned him into "last year's model."

One Last Thought

If there is one thread that weaves itself through the lives of Wilbur and Orville Wright, it was their insatiable curiosity to understand the things around them. It was curiosity that drove them to understand the toy helicopter their father gave to them as boys. It was embedded in their desire to understand how birds could change direction in flight. It was in their interest in knowing about the world about them. It was the force that fueled their drive to understand, then conquer, the problem of flight. Eric Hoffer once said, "Learners inherit the future." In the case of Wilbur and Orville Wright, relentless preparation, or the problem-solving principle of forever learning, enabled them to "inherit the wind."

Neither Wilbur nor Orville would ever lose his curiosity about the things around them, or lessen his commitment to forever learning. This was never more evident than in the weeks leading up to Orville's historic first flight on December 17, 1903, as indicated in the comments Orville makes, either in his diary or in letters to his sister Katharine at home:

November 1, 1903
We are highly pleased with our progress so far this year. I have been putting in about an hour every night in studying German.

November 12, 1903
After four or five flights we took the machine back to camp. Spent most of afternoon in chopping wood and reading.

November 15, 1903
I am taking up my French and German again and making some progress.

December 13, 1903
Spent most of the day (Sunday) reading.

You would think that trying to solve the problem of heavier-than-air flight would be enough to fill anyone's mind. Yet, up to just four days before his historic flight, Orville was still filling his mind with knowledge. When asked to describe his son Orville, Bishop Wright once commented, "His mind grew steadily." Michelangelo would have been proud.

CHAPTER EIGHT

MEASURE TWICE

THE PRINCIPLE OF METHODICAL METICULOUSNESS

*We could not help thinking that many of their troubles
might have been avoided and that others might have been
overcome by the adoption of more adequate methods.*

Wilbur Wright

MEASURE TWICE is a problem-solving principle that says the fastest and
most efficient way to solve a problem is by being meticulous and methodical in your approach.

*   *   *

The Paul Laurence Dunbar Library on the campus of Wright State
University houses the largest collection of Wright brothers materials outside of the Library of Congress in Washington, D.C. Included in the collection, which contains more than 6,000 items, are hundreds of
photographs taken by Wilbur and Orville Wright during the course of the
work on their flying machine. The use of photography to record and document their research was a deliberate part of the Wright brothers' strategy,

serving both historical and scientific purposes. Along with the brothers' correspondence, notebooks, and personal diaries, these photographs make the world's first heavier-than-air flying machine one of the best-documented inventions in history.

While doing some of my research at the library, I took a break to stretch my legs. After examining a full-size reproduction of the *Wright Flyer* suspended gracefully from the library's ceiling, I noticed a number of display cases lining one of the walls. One of the cases contained an impressive array of medals and medallions, honors bestowed on the Wright brothers by kings and heads of state. Another contained some of the original books recommended by the Smithsonian Institution in response to Wilbur's inquiry and purchased by the Wright brothers in June 1899. I noticed that Wilbur had penciled notes in the margin of one of the books, a habit of mine as well. There was one display case, however, that intrigued me the most.

An Interesting Case . . .

The case that captured my interest contained a small diary and a first-generation photograph of Orville's historic flight. The diary was one of many kept by the Wright brothers' father, Bishop Milton Wright. The Bishop was an avid diarist who kept track of his day's events for over sixty years. In 1999, Wright State University Libraries catalogued and published the journals as *Diaries 1857–1917,* putting sixty years of Wright family history in a concise, readable format. "The Bishop's diaries," notes Tom Crouch in the book's introduction, "offer an invaluable window into a household where history was made."

The diary in the display case was open to the Bishop's entry for Thursday, December 17, 1903. Of the thousands of entries the Bishop had made in his journals over his long life and career, the one he made this day must have been the most satisfying. With clear, firm penmanship, Bishop Wright had written:

> In the afternoon about 5:30, we received the following telegram from Orville, dated Kitty Hawk, N.C., Dec. 17. "Bishop M. Wright: Success four flights Thursday morning all against a twenty-one

mile wind started from level with engine power alone average speed through the air thirty-one miles—longest 57 seconds. XXX home Christmas. Orville Wright."

In reading other entries from *Diaries,* I was surprised at the detail Bishop Wright captures in such small spaces. Some entries were humorous, such as his indignation at having to pay the exorbitant price of $1 for breakfast during one of his many extended trips. Others were poignant, such as his entry for Thursday, June 6, 1912. Following his son Wilbur's death from typhoid fever a week earlier, the Bishop wrote, "I felt Wilbur's absence as never before." Regardless of the sentiment or subject of the entry, the reader of the journals can't help but be impressed by the Bishop's methodical and meticulous capture of detail.

Just Point and Shoot

In aviation circles, the first-flight photograph of Orville Wright, the other item in the display case, is referred to simply as The Shot. Regarded by many as the most famous photograph in aviation history (it's certainly the most reproduced), the picture captures the moment the *Wright Flyer* lifts off its starting track. The photograph, which yields an enormous amount of information, is one of the most thoroughly analyzed pictures of all time. One group of researchers, by examining the blur pattern of the propellers, was able to determine the stop setting of the camera used to take it. Now that's meticulous!

Many think the photograph was a "lucky shot," as if the photography gods were smiling on Kill Devil Hills that day.

I've seen the picture many times. In fact, it appears in half a dozen Wright brothers posters displayed in my office. Looking at a first-generation copy, however, was almost hypnotic. The picture is perfectly framed, not only catching Orville lying "bellybumpums" (an Outer Banks phrase) on the flyer, but Wilbur running alongside in midstride. There is a good deal of poetic justice in the fact that both brothers are in the picture. What makes this photograph truly remarkable, however, is that it's the *only shot* of this historic moment. It was taken with a view camera set up and loaded for one exposure only, to be snapped by a man who had never

taken a picture before in his life, and would never do so again. Pretty for-
tuitous, wouldn't you say?

Many think the photograph was a "lucky shot," as if the photography
gods were smiling on Kill Devil Hills that day. The shot was anything but
accidental, however, a point Orville went out of his way to make in his
book, *How We Invented the Airplane.* Seneca, the ancient Roman philosopher, said that luck is what happens when preparation meets opportunity.
On the morning of December 17, 1903, after the *Wright Flyer* had been
placed on its starting track (the brothers liked to call it the Grand Junction
Railroad), Orville picked up his anemometer and checked the wind speed.
He already knew the amount of thrust his motor and propellers would give
him, so given his considerable mathematical skill, it was easy to calculate
the point where the machine would become airborne. With a 25 mph
wind, Orville knew in advance that he would not need the entire track.

Orville placed the wooden tripod behind and slightly to the right of
the *Flyer,* then set his camera in place. He adjusted it until it faced the
spot on the monorail where he believed the flyer would lift off. John
Daniels, one of the surfmen from the Kill Devil Hills Lifesaving Station
who had come over to offer assistance, was pulled aside by Orville and
given instructions on how to take the photograph. His role was reduced
to triggering the shutter when the flyer rose a foot or two off its launch
rail, then putting the plate back in the camera. Daniels deserves credit for
squeezing the bulb at the right moment, but that's all. The bulk of the
credit for this historic photograph goes to Orville for his meticulous
attention to detail, for being prepared for his opportunity.

A Common Thread

What do the diaries of Bishop Wright and the photograph of Orville's first
flight have in common? For one thing, they both capture the history of
December 17, 1903. But they capture something else as well: the family's
penchant for paying close attention to detail. It is a mental discipline that
would play a significant role in the Wright brothers' work, emerging in
my research as a problem-solving principle I call *methodical meticulousness.* It was an important trait that would guide the brothers systemati-
cally through the problem, allowing them not only to solve it, but to solve

it economically and expeditiously. Surprisingly, it was not a discipline practiced by many of their peers in early aviation.

Most of those attacking the problem of heavier-than-air powered flight were doing so in what author Peter Jakab called a "mercurial and haphazard" manner. A considerable amount of time and money, not to mention opportunity for success, was being squandered by quixotic "trial and error" approaches. The goal for most aviation pioneers was to get their machines in the air, then they'd worry about the rest later. The Wright brothers, however, had little interest in performing a flying stunt. They were interested in understanding every element of the problem in an effort to produce a replicable process.

Measure Twice

Measure twice (cut once) is a problem-solving principle that states that the fastest and most efficient way to get to the solution of any problem is by being *methodical* and *meticulous* in addressing it. Speed and accuracy come from taking the time to do the necessary "foundation work" early on, to eliminate having to repeat or retrace earlier steps. For many, meticulousness and speed seem a contradiction, but simple errors and oversights made in an effort to save time are much more costly than committing the time up-front to give careful attention to detail. The goal of meticulousness is accuracy, but speed, surprisingly, is one of its by-products.

> The goal of meticulousness is accuracy, but speed, surprisingly, is one of its by-products.

Being methodical and meticulous in their work was not simply the result of anal-retentive personalities. The Wright brothers were, to be sure, disciplined and analytical thinkers. Their meticulousness, however, was born of the need to accomplish three objectives in their work:

➤ *Use time efficiently.* Time was a significant factor for the brothers, and not just because they were in a race to be the first to fly. Wilbur and Orville were unable to justify working full-time on something that might never amount to anything more than a hobby. Fortunately, the seasonal nature of their bicycle business gave them time in the winter to work on the problem. The Wright brothers' "need for speed" was facilitated by their passion for getting things right the first time . . . to save time later on.

➤ *Use money effectively.* "With little money to spend on a hobby," biographer Fred Kelly says of the Wright brothers, "it was cheaper to rectify mistakes on paper." Unlike Samuel Langley and Clément Ader, who were able to raise significant funding from government sources, the Wright brothers were paying for their work out of the profits generated from their bicycle business. They could not afford to waste a penny, and mistakes cost money. Their methodical and meticulous approach allowed them to reduce errors and save money.

➤ *Maximize personal safety.* As important as time and money were to the Wright brothers, neither was as critical as personal safety. "The man who wishes to keep at the problem long enough to really learn something," Wilbur wrote his father in 1900, "positively must not take dangerous risks." Wilbur's concerns were not limited to foolish risk taking. "Carelessness and overconfidence," he said, "are usually more dangerous than deliberately accepted risks."

For Wilbur and Orville, who would put their time, money, and personal safety on the line in attacking the problem of heavier-than-air flight, meticulous and methodical research was the antidote to overconfidence and carelessness. More than a character trait, attention to detail was a problem-solving principle that put precision ahead of guesswork, something neither of the brothers could tolerate.

Breaking It Down

For the purpose of illustrating this problem-solving principle, I've broken the concept of methodical meticulousness into individual components, much as the Wright brothers would do whenever they addressed a problem or issue. The components are: planning and preparation, attention to detail, subsetting, and detailed record keeping. Taken together, these four activities gave the Wright brothers a decided edge in the race to invent the world's first heavier-than-air flying machine. The principle can do the same for businesses today.

Planning and Preparation

When Wilbur wrote a letter to the Smithsonian Institution on May 30, 1899, requesting aeronautical information, he stated his intentions upfront. "I intend," he wrote, "to begin a systematic study of the subject in preparation for practical work." For the Wright brothers, preparation—or early planning—was the starting point of all endeavors. Although completely capable of thinking "outside the box," both men knew that structure and organization were essential ingredients in unraveling the secrets of flight. They knew it was an extraordinarily complex problem, and they sought first to lay a firm foundation for their work.

The beginning point for the Wrights was to define the problem before them. Many of those who had taken on the challenge of heavier-than-air flight, and failed, could trace the origin of their failure to a poorly defined problem. Early flying-machine pioneers such as Ader, Langley, and Hiram Maxim had defined the problem simply: They were attempting "to fly." As a result, the focus of their efforts was on getting their machines in the air. Wilbur and Orville, on the other hand, defined the problem as flying "balanced and under control." It was a minor difference with major consequences, pointing the brothers in an entirely different direction. Correctly defining the problem was an essential first step for the Wright brothers, one repeated each time they confronted a new issue.

Wilbur and Orville were crisp, logical thinkers who would not begin work on any problem without solid planning and preparation. In *Visions of a Flying Machine*, Peter Jakab writes, "They readily recognized the wisdom of comparatively mundane, incremental steps over bold, all-or-nothing attempts to fly." It seems like an obvious starting point, but the Wright brothers were about the only ones who did practical planning and preparation. In many respects, they were just following their mother's advice.

Attention to Detail

Carroll Glines, in *The Wright Brothers: Pioneers of Power Flight,* tells a story of Susan Koerner Wright's attention to detail. With money and material in short supply, the Wright brothers' mother was careful not to waste either. An excellent seamstress and designer, she had a routine she followed when making a new dress. Before putting scissors to fabric, she created—and tried on—a paper pattern of the dress. Once she confirmed a proper fit, she transferred the pattern to the material and began cutting. Glines recounts a story where Susan tells her sons, "Make your mistakes on paper if you can." We don't know if she said those exact words, but it's not hard to imagine her demonstrating that sentiment. It didn't take Wilbur long to learn the lesson.

In July 1885, Bishop Wright started a weekly newspaper called *The Christian Conservator* and hired Wilbur to fold the eight-page publication as it came off the press. The job was repetitive and boring, two things any boy would hate. As he continued to suffer through the boredom and tediousness of folding the papers, Wilbur began to consider ways to automate the process. He began, as his mother had taught him, by sketching out plans for a folding machine. Once the plans were complete, he knew exactly what he needed to build it. Using the treadle from an old sewing machine and other parts he could round up, Wilbur was able to invent a folding machine that reduced the time needed to do the job by fifty percent. Susan's "pattern" of meticulousness was transferred to her sons. It would one day be transferred to a flying machine.

My friend Bill may be the most methodical and meticulous person I know, a good trait for a chief financial officer. His commitment to accuracy, however, extended well beyond the crunching of numbers. By encouraging everyone in his company to take a little care in how they did their jobs, he single-handedly managed to influence corporate culture with his passion for paying attention to detail. Although he didn't originate the phrase, "measure twice, cut once" was his mantra. As a result of Bill's watchfulness (we jokingly called it "mothering"), everyone in the company began paying closer attention to their work. The company went "un-dinged" (no violations) by ISO auditors for ten years thanks to Bill's challenge to do it right the first time. Every company needs a champion like Bill.

Subsetting

It was a dreary, rainy day when I visited the Wright Cycle Company in Dayton, where, from 1895 to 1897, the Wright brothers conducted their bicycle business. The building, the last original remaining site in Dayton related to the Wright brothers, is now under the direction of the National Park Service. Because of the weather, I was the only person in the museum that day. I had the park ranger, a man knowledgeable about the Wright brothers, all to myself and took advantage of the opportunity. During our conversation, I asked my guide if he were to pick one trait above all others that allowed the Wright brothers to succeed where so many had failed, what he would choose. Rubbing his salt-and-pepper beard for a moment, he replied, "I think it was their ability to take a complex problem and break it down into manageable components."

The ranger's advice reminded me of a former math professor of mine who always said the easiest way to eat an elephant was one bite at a time! Taken in its entirety, the problem of manned, heavier-than-air flight was one overwhelming "elephant." The Wright brothers, in taking on the challenge, were not overwhelmed by the whole, since they chose from the beginning to break the problem into manageable components, working on the most important problems, "the tyrants," first (see Chapter 4).

The Wright brothers invented their flying machine by solving a number of smaller problems.

Plutarch, the Greek philosopher, once wrote: "Many things which cannot be overcome when they are together, yield themselves up when taken little by little." It's interesting to note that Plutarch was Wilbur's favorite writer.

In *Visions of a Flying Machine,* Peter Jakab writes, "Wilbur and Orville understood that the airplane is not a single device, but a series of discrete mechanical and structural entities that, when working in unison, resulted in a machine capable of flight." Although the Wright brothers are credited with inventing the world's first heavier-than-air flying machine, what they really invented was:

- Wing-warping (a method for lateral control)
- A forward elevator (a method to control pitch)
- A wind tunnel (to create the first accurate body of aeronautical data)
- A movable single rudder (a method to control yaw)
- A propeller (an efficient method of creating thrust)
- The science of flight

The Wright brothers invented their flying machine by solving a number of smaller problems that, when taken as a whole, yielded the solution to heavier-than-air powered flight. It was considerably easier to invent the components of a flying machine. It was all a part of their strategy to move through the problem as methodically as possible. Nowhere was that strategy more in evidence than during their wind tunnel tests in the winter of 1901.

Detailed Record Keeping

Accuracy was the passion of Orville's professional life. Legend has it that in an effort to bring order to the kitchen of their Kill Devil Hills camp, he numbered eggs so they could be eaten in the same sequence in which they had been laid. Whether it's true or not, the story seems apt, given Orville's attention to detail. Wilbur was just as precise. Their penchant for exactness would be put to good use when the brothers conducted their glide experiments in 1901. Over two hundred glides were made that season, with the information on each flight—its duration, distance covered, and angle of incidence—carefully captured and logged. The brothers then reexamined their data in lab experiments the winter following those glides.

What Was That All About?

The gliding season of 1901 on the Outer Banks had been a considerable disappointment. Despite their best efforts, the brothers could not get their glider to perform as expected. After several weeks of frustration, they suspended manned glides altogether, spending their last week before heading home tinkering with the front elevator and flying the glider as a kite. With the time of their departure at hand, Wilbur decided to make one last attempt. The glider was carried to the top of Big Hill, the largest of three sand dunes that faced their campsite, where Wilbur climbed aboard. It was a beautiful day to fly.

As soon as he was airborne, Wilbur encountered what he later described as a "peculiar feeling of instability." When he tried to warp the wings, the glider seemed to develop a mind of its own (Wilbur's description), darting alarmingly toward the ground. Wilbur's countermeasures were to no effect. As the left wing skimmed the top of the dune, the glider spun out of control and slammed into the ground. Wilbur was pitched headlong into the forward elevator, suffering cuts, bruises, and a black eye. For the first time during the course of their research, the Wright brothers experienced a feeling not felt before: genuine fear. It was justified. The circumstances of Wilbur's crash were the same as the ones that had killed Otto Lilienthal and Percy Pilcher.

Orville later recalled that he and Wilbur left Kill Devil Hills in August 1901 "muddled and confused." At the center of their confusion was the fact that their glider had failed to generate the amount of lift their calculations predicted. The brothers had designed both their 1900 and 1901 gliders using air pressure tables published by Lilienthal in the 1896 edition of the Smithsonian's *Aeronautical Annuals*. Now they were beginning to suspect the tables, long accepted as accurate by aviation pioneers, might be in error. Wilbur later recalled the moment:

> We saw that the calculations upon which all flying machines had been based were unreliable, and that all were simply groping in the dark. Having set out with absolute faith in existing scientific data, we were driven to doubt one thing after another, till finally, after two years of experiment, we cast it all aside, and decided to rely entirely on our own investigations.

It was a tough situation for the brothers, whose respect for the German engineer was considerable. It was Lilienthal who had inspired Wilbur and Orville to take up the challenge of heavier-than-air manned flight. Now they found themselves on the verge of discrediting his work. But the brothers had a low tolerance for error, and no interest whatsoever in risking their lives on questionable data. Lilienthal's numbers had to be verified. The question was, how?

As usual, the first step for the Wright brothers in addressing any problem was to think it through, theorizing on the possibilities. The brothers' real objective was not only to prove or disprove Lilienthal's tables, but also to determine the correct information that would lead to the development of the correct wing camber (i.e., curvature). After consideration, the brothers decided that the starting point was to check the airfoil (i.e., wing) design used by Lilienthal in determining his tables.

Deciding that Lilienthal's method of testing, which relied on a whirling arm with airfoils attached, was inefficient, the brothers came up with the idea of attaching a miniature version of Lilienthal's airfoil on a bicycle wheel mounted horizontally in front of the handlebars of a bicycle. By riding the bicycle at a set speed—both with and against the wind, to factor out variances—they were able to prove that a problem with Lilienthal's numbers did exist. They had measured once, and now they would measure again.

To verify (i.e., measure twice) the information from their bicycle test, Orville decided to build a makeshift wind tunnel. Using a discarded wooden starch box and a fan driven off the overhead drive shaft that powered other tools in their shop, Orville was able to generate a flow of air that could be used to measure the effects of the wind on the various shapes placed inside the wind tunnel. A piece of glass in the top of the crate allowed him to observe the reaction of the airfoils to the wind. The tunnel was in use for only a day, but it was all the time needed to confirm the discrepancies in Lilienthal's data. To get the kind of specificity they now needed would require a wind tunnel much more sophisticated than their present version.

(Wind) Tunnel Vision

If December 17, 1903, qualifies as the most important date in aviation history, November 22, 1901, would have to be the second. That was the day the Wright brothers completed work on their new wind tunnel and began making the measurements and calculations that would unravel the mystery of flight. The first time I saw a replica of the Wright brothers' wind tunnel at the National Air and Space Museum at Wright-Patterson Air Force Base, I was surprised at its crude simplicity. To the untrained eye, it looks like a long wooden crate sitting on top of a few sawhorses. With this instrument, however, the Wright brothers would solve the problem of flight. "They generated all the information they would need," writes Fred Culick in *On Great White Wings*, "to design airplanes and propellers for the rest of their lives."

It was difficult for me to appreciate the significance of this crude-looking testing device since I spent the better portion of my career in the electronics industry calling on design engineers. Whenever I had the

opportunity to tour their labs, I was always impressed by the sophistication of the equipment used to test the accuracy of their work. Fluke mul-
timeters, Tektronix oscilloscopes, and HP signal generators were always
in evidence. When I saw the replica of the wind tunnel at the Air and
Space Museum, the magnitude of its contribution to solving the problem
of heavier-than-air flight escaped me. I soon learned that its exalted position among the discoveries that led to flight was well justified.

The Answer's Blowin' in the Wind

One of the critical needs of a wind tunnel is that the stream of air passing through it has to be smooth and steady. If it caroms off the walls
inside, it creates anomalies that will distort the data. Orville solved the
problem by placing a honeycomb-shaped baffle in front of the fan, which
straightened the flow. On the top, at the opposite end of the fan, Orville
placed a glass window, which allowed him to observe the action inside
while the fan was running. At the heart of this
instrument was a simple but ingenious set of balances that allowed the brothers to mount a variety of airfoils (i.e., wing models). Fashioned out
of bicycle spokes and hacksaw blades, the balances were a creative marvel that allowed the
brothers to make setups fairly quickly.

Over a period of two
months, Wilbur
and Orville would
methodically set up
and measure nearly
two hundred models.

On the two balances, one to measure lift and the other drift, Wilbur
and Orville were able to mount a series of metal strips shaped like wings.
If you can imagine looking at the cross section of an airplane wing, you
will be able to visualize the shape of these airfoil models. Using tin shears,
the brothers cut sheet metal into strips about six inches long. These were
then hammered into shapes with the curvature they desired. Sometimes
solder and wax were added to the strips to create different designs. Over
a period of two months, Wilbur and Orville would methodically set up
and measure nearly two hundred models, meticulously recording the data
into their logbook. It was painstaking and tedious, but the brothers found
the work intellectually stimulating. In remembering those hectic days,
Orville said, "Wilbur and I could hardly wait for morning to come to get
at something that interested us. That's happiness!"

As the brothers began to retrieve the data from their wind tunnel, they were able to prove two things. The first was that Otto Lilienthal's tables were incorrect. Second, the reason Lilienthal's data were incorrect was because one of the coefficients he was using was wrong. Lilienthal created his table using the long-accepted value for air pressure, called Smeaton's Coefficient, which was 0.005. Using their wind tunnel, the Wright brothers were able to prove that the real number was closer to 0.0033. When they recalculated Lilienthal's numbers using the new numbers, the brothers knew beyond a doubt why their gliders of 1900 and 1901 had responded so poorly. Neither had sufficient wing size to generate the needed lift.

Pulling the numbers off their wind tunnel was only half the battle. Those numbers also had to be plugged into geometric and trigonometric formulas to calculate the data needed for new tables on lift and drag. It was tedious and time-consuming work that the brothers continued until December 31, 1901. Knowing that the bicycle business was their livelihood and that the products they would offer for sale in the spring needed to be built the preceding winter, the brothers had the discipline to walk away from their passion. It was, after all, only a hobby.

The Need for Speed

One of the extraordinary features of the Wright brothers' solution to the problem of heavier-than-air manned flight is the speed in which it unraveled. As we've seen, it was only fifty-five months from the time they first considered the problem until the time they flew. By today's standards, that's a long time to bring out a new product. But in 1900, it was operating at the speed of blur. People had been working on the problem for centuries without success. The Wright brothers come along and solve the problem in a little over four years' time. It gets better.

The Wright brothers actually had the solution to flight when they completed their wind tunnel tests in the winter of 1901. The glider they would produce in 1902, which was based on the wind tunnel data, would become the basis for their successful patent application for a flying machine. Unbelievably, that glider, which featured the Wright brothers' remarkable wing-warping control system, was constructed from materials that had been available for over a hundred years. The two years from its development until it was actually flown as a powered glider was largely spent learning how to fly.

The Wright brothers were able to move so quickly because of their meticulous and methodical approach to the problem. Instead of slowing them down, their meticulousness removed many of the time-wasters known to any project: backtracking, reworking, and procrastination. Having a detailed plan to follow, then working the plan, is still the fastest approach to a solution. Many of those who believe "thinking on your feet" or "winging it" is the best approach to problem solving are still trying to get their ideas off the ground. If speed to market is an issue in your organization, take a good hard look at the measure twice principle.

Learning to Soar

Here are a few tips to guide you as you make measure twice, or methodical meticulousness, a part of the problem-solving process in your company or organization:

- *Make a commitment to accuracy a part of your organization's culture.* Practices tend to become part of a company's culture when leaders and managers talk about them. Make it a point to reinforce your company's commitment to accuracy by referencing it in mission and core value statements, as well as in daily comments made in meetings or on the shop floor. Assumptions, as everybody knows, can be costly.

- *Emphasize that speed is a function of accuracy.* The Wright brothers solved the problem of heavier-than-air manned flight in just fifty-five months. Since speed is interdependent with accuracy, nothing is lost in the speed-to-market sector by being methodical and meticulous. Indeed, much is gained.

- *Keep extraordinary records when preplanning.* Successful brainstorming requires an unstructured environment where participants can freewheel their way through a problem. But unless the ideas are captured in a formal (i.e., structured) way, the process may end up being nothing more than a stimulating chat. Not only does meticulous note-taking track progress, it provides a useful roadmap for those times when it's necessary to backtrack.

➻ *Measure twice, cut once.* Nothing steals more time and money from an organization than mistakes. Small or large, most mistakes can be eliminated by simply double-checking the work for accuracy. It's a piece of advice carpenters live by, and so should we.

➻ *Keep a roots log.* A company I worked for made a point of entering the results of every meeting in something it called a "roots log." Every major achievement, every problem overcome, every new strategy implemented—all were meticulously recorded. On more than a few occasions, even years after the event, the material we had carefully captured was able to assist us.

➻ *Create subsets of the problem.* Break the problem down into manageable components. A problem "as big as a house" can be more easily entered by finding an "open window." Breaking problems into subsets is the equivalent of finding that window.

➻ *Teach your employees that meticulousness is a creative process, too.* Some people think that being vigilant in order to minimize errors prevents them from being as creative as they might be. Great ideas need landing gear as well as wings. Being methodical and meticulous helps translate out-of-the-box thinking into practical steps to be followed.

➻ *Practice kaizen. Kaizen* is a Japanese word meaning continual improvement. Not great leaps forward, as Chairman Mao advocated, but gradual and orderly improvement. A methodical approach that identifies waste and error may well be the fastest way to the goal.

➻ *Lay a solid foundation.* Begin the problem-solving process by (1) correctly defining the problem, (2) determining what's needed (e.g., information, tools, people) to solve it, and (3) developing a plan to secure the needed resources. A solid foundation will ensure that what's built upon it will endure. "In any enterprise," the Roman writer Publius Syrius said, "consider first where you want to come out."

How accurate were the Wright brothers? Many of their concepts are still in use a hundred years later. As a result of their meticulous approach to the problem of heavier-than-air powered flight, the Wright brothers had recorded everything. They knew exactly what they did. They knew exactly when they did it. They knew how they did it. They knew why they did it. The information would be invaluable years later in defending their patents in court.

The search for excellence is the search for accuracy.

In many companies, the mantra of "get it right the first time" has been replaced with "just get it done." The search for excellence, however, is the search for accuracy. Few companies, it seems, realize that accuracy is at the root of competitive advantage. Service excellence, superior products, profitability—all are the result of individuals doing their work accurately every step of the way, from conception and design to production and shipment. Companies placing an emphasis on accurate (i.e., clear, detailed, specific, distinct, correct) work are the ones most likely to get their ideas off the ground.

One Last Thought

In preparation for this book, I bought several models of the 1903 *Wright Flyer.* I wanted to understand all the features of this remarkable invention, and I thought handling the components and seeing how they fit together would help me to better understand what Wilbur and Orville had accomplished. As I laid the parts out on the table, I was surprised at how many little pieces there were. Without consulting the directions (I think they call it "flying by the seat of your pants"), I began snapping a few of the larger pieces together. There's something inherently satisfying about working with big pieces because you can see the progress you're making. I was anxious to see the model start looking like a plane. Satisfied with the snap fit, I took them apart and applied the glue. "Now we're making progress," I thought.

While the glue was drying on the larger part, I decided it was a good time to paint some of the smaller pieces. I picked up the little model of Orville lying in a prone position, applied black paint to his coat, hat, and trousers, then set him aside to dry, too. I proceeded in this fashion for about an hour, then set my project aside. When I returned a couple of days later, everything had dried or set up as expected. Unsure of what came next, I picked up the directions. The first thing I read was: "Don't paint anything until first glued in place." The paint, I learned, keeps the glue from sticking. I now had my model of the *Wright Flyer,* only "Orville" kept rolling off it. That wasn't the end of my problems, however. The rest of the instructions carried a warning that said something to this effect: "Do not glue the big pieces together before putting the smaller ones in place." I eventually got my model together, and even learned a good deal about the inventive process of the original flyer, but not without a lot of rework and delay.

The fact of the matter is, meticulousness is not my default position. I'm a "big picture" person who likes to push a project along. There's a time and place for that approach, but not every time and not every place. The meticulousness of Orville and the methodical approach of Wilbur have taught me that there are many aspects of my life and work that will profit if I pay attention to detail. I'm not signing up for any twelve-step programs, but improvement is at the top of my list. There's a lot of benefit to be gained somewhere between marking your eggs and not reading the directions.

CHAPTER NINE

FORCE MULTIPLICATION

THE PRINCIPLE OF TEAM EQUITY

They (Wilbur and Orville) are equal in their inven-
tions, neither claiming any superiority above the other,
nor accepting any honor to the neglect of the other.
Neither could have mastered the problem alone.

Bishop Milton Wright (1828–1917)

FORCE MULTIPLICATION is a problem-solving principle stating that the output of a group of people (force) with a common purpose is increased exponentially (multiplied) by a seamless interdependence powered by five areas of team equity: trust, effort, profits, power, and honor.

*   *   *

The Wright brothers may have worked in obscurity at the beginning of the twentieth century, but by 1910 they were two of the most famous people in the world. Photographers in Europe, as well as in America, loved snapping Wilbur and Orville, and pictures of the brothers abounded. Today, the Special Collections and Archives section of the Wright State University Libraries has more than 4,000 photographs documenting the invention of heavier-than-air powered flight, as well as the lives of the Wright family. The Library of Congress has many more. The photographs provide a fascinating look into the men and the times and give the story a depth and dimension that would otherwise be missing. Although the photograph of the first flight is the most examined and recognized image, my personal favorite is one taken of the brothers in October 1910 on Long Island, New York.

The photograph, taken at Belmont Park during the International Aviation Tournament, epitomizes the working relationship of the brothers. The photograph offers a visual illustration of how well the two men, different in so many respects, were able to blend their personalities in pursuit of a common objective. In the picture, the men are dressed nearly identically, both wearing dark three-piece suits and sporting trademark bowler hats. Their strides are matched, each stepping forward confidently with left foot extended, the toes of their shoes turned up at the same angle. Similar in physical stature (Wilbur was an inch or two taller), the only thing that spoils the symmetry of the photograph is the coat draped over Orville's arm. It's a photograph of two men in sync.

There are many aspects of the Wright brothers' story that are remarkable, but none more than the working relationship of Wilbur and Orville. I like to call it Team Wright. Their partnership, perhaps the greatest inventive collaboration in history, is worth a closer look. How could two people who were so different function so seamlessly? With all the baggage that a sibling relationship can carry, how were they able to achieve such a degree of compatibility? How were two strong-willed men, with deeply held opinions on how things should be done, able to consistently find areas of agreement? How did two people who frequently engaged each other in heated argument avoid the destructive residue of those encounters?

Wright biographer Harry Combs describes the relationship of Wilbur and Orville as nothing short of miraculous. "We have another miracle," Combs writes in *Kill Devil Hill: Discovering the Secret of the Wright Brothers*, "in that these two men . . . worked so closely, fitted their minds so intimately, formed so total a rapport with one another, that history records their accomplishments as the work and effort of a single entity." Extraordinary to be sure, but not miraculous. To call the success of Team

Wright miraculous implies that it's something unachievable under normal circumstances, leading us away from the ingredients that made their partnership work—ingredients that can be used today to develop a highly effective team.

"It is unlikely," Peter Jakab writes in *Vision of a Flying Machine,* "that either Wilbur or Orville could have achieved alone what they did as a team." Although Wilbur was the first to have an interest in the flying problem, he quickly realized he could not solve it by himself. "The problem is too great," he wrote in a letter to aviation expert Octave Chanute in 1900, "for one man alone to solve in secret." He recruited the best partner he knew, his brother Orville. Together, they would develop a creative energy that would grow in force and magnitude. The equity of that relationship was never more clearly demonstrated than it was during a common decision-making exercise, one we've all employed on occasion. It took place on the sandy plains of Kill Devil Hills in the winter of 1903.

The First Attempt

The days leading up to the brothers' first attempt at powered flight on December 14, 1903, had been challenging ones. Nagging problems, such as a sprocket that kept working itself loose, had frustrated their progress. A bent propeller shaft had forced Orville to rush back to Dayton to personally oversee the manufacture of its replacement. He returned to Kitty Hawk on December 11, and by the following morning, the shaft was in place. They were ready to go. Unusually calm winds that day, however, prevented their making an attempt. Since the brothers refused to work on the Sabbath out of respect for their father, Sunday, December 13, was a day of rest and reading. Later that afternoon, Adam Ethridge from the Kill Devil Hills Lifesaving Station brought his wife, Lillie, and their children to the Wright brothers' camp to see their flying machine. It was evidence of his belief that something special was about to occur. On Monday, the brothers were ready to fly.

If a person were looking for a defining moment in the Wright brothers' partnership, it occurred the afternoon of December 14, 1903. The morning that day was calm, and the brothers were unsure about making an attempt to fly. But they were growing uncharacteristically impatient, and around 1:00 P.M. they decided to "have a whack." Orville climbed a ladder to the top of their hangar and tacked a red flag in place, a prearranged signal to alert the surfmen at the lifesaving station they were about to attempt a flight. Half an hour later, five lifesavers and a couple of children strolled into camp to offer assistance.

The surfmen at the Kill Devil Hills and Kitty Hawk Lifesaving Stations had assisted the Wright brothers for four years, offering help on a volunteer basis. They offered their assistance for two reasons. First, duty as a lifesaver along the rugged Atlantic rim could get pretty boring, and the Wright brothers were decent entertainment. Where else could you find two men, dressed every day in clothes that Outer Bankers reserved for Sunday, throwing themselves off the side of a big dune in a flying contraption? Second, they'd taken a liking to the two "odd ducks" from Dayton. Their help was appreciated. Wilbur and Orville not only needed assistance hauling their 700-pound flyer up Big Kill Devil Hill, they needed witnesses should the flight be a success.

With the flyer in place and preflight checks complete, the brothers took their places in front of the two propellers. On count, each gave his respective propeller a sharp downward thrust. As the engine cracked and popped to life, frightened children and a dog ran for cover. While the little twelve-horsepower engine was warming up, Wilbur and Orville drew aside from the others. One of the brothers, probably Wilbur, reached into his pocket, pulled out a coin, and flipped it into the air. The coin was caught and turned onto a wrist. The removal of a hand revealed which brother would have the honor of making the first attempt to fly.

Call It!

It's ironic that these men, so methodical and meticulous in all they did, would make one of the most important decisions in aviation history in such fashion. Can you imagine Neil Armstrong and Buzz Aldrin facing each other in their Apollo Lunar Module and "counting potatoes" (a flipped coin would float away!) to see who would be the first to set foot on the moon? Although historians agree that Orville's participation was crucial, most believe that Wilbur was the driving force behind their effort. It was Wilbur who first had the idea of attacking the flying problem. It was Wilbur who took the initiative in getting information from the Smithsonian Institution needed to get their study under way. It was Wilbur who conceived the concept of wing-warping that was critical to providing lateral equilibrium (i.e., control) during flight.

By all rights, many say, Wilbur deserved to make the first attempt. Even Orville said as much. But Wilbur would have it no other way. The brothers had labored side-by-side for fifty-five months in an intensive effort to solve the problem of heavier-than-air flight. In Wilbur's eyes, it made little difference whether one was a "shooter" or "ammo carrier," both were essential to victory. Wilbur might have remembered the winter of 1901 when he had been so discouraged with their work that he wanted to quit. Orville, ever the optimist, had pulled his brother out of the doldrums and back on track. Wilbur knew the *Wright Flyer* had both their fingerprints all over it, and that the only equitable way to decide who would have the honor of the first attempt was a coin toss. And equity was crucial to their collaboration.

> The only equitable way to decide who would have the honor of the first attempt was a coin toss.

The Forces of (Human) Nature

In many respects, the story of the Wright brothers is about force: identifying it, calculating its impact, harnessing its power. Although most people recognize the Wright brothers as the inventors of the world's first practical flying machine, few realize that they invented the science of flight as well. The process of coming to understand the vagaries of aerodynamics was a critical part of their research and a frequent topic of discussion in their debates. For example, to design the correct curvature of an airfoil or calculate the square footage of a wing surface, the brothers had to address the forces of lift and drag. Atmospheric forces such as gravity and resistance affected the design of everything from engine size (weight and horsepower) to propeller length and curvature. Wilbur and Orville knew that the interaction of these forces, once understood and mastered, would yield the solution to manned flight.

No force, however, had a greater impact on the success of the Wright brothers than that created by the power of their collaborative effort. Like the factors in Einstein's theory of relativity, the brothers seemed to interact in a way that caused their output to increase exponentially. I call it the principle of *force multiplication*. Although *synergy* is a popular (if not overused) word to describe teamwork, it falls short in defining the concept I'm talking about. Synergy simply means that the sum of the parts exceeds the whole. With force multiplication, the sum of the parts not only exceeds the whole, it does so in ever-increasing fashion. The teamwork of the Wright brothers allowed Wilbur and Orville to advance their knowledge and understanding exponentially.

Force Multiplication

It's important to note that the principle here is not teamwork, but force multiplication. The team, a group of people working together to achieve common goals, is the force. The effectiveness of that force can be multiplied in ever-increasing fashion when care is taken to keep its key components—its core equities—in balance. The team's equities are those components that determine and measure its ability to function in a fair and just manner. When equities are carefully monitored and balanced, the team no longer functions individually, or even synergistically. It functions exponentially, continually multiplying its effectiveness and impact.

A classic example of force multiplication in Team Wright occurred during the brothers' gliding experiments in 1902. As mentioned in Chapter 3, the glides were going well, except that one out of every fifty or so flights would stall out, resulting in a heart-stopping plunge to the earth. As was their style, the brothers debated the issue furiously one evening before going to bed. Instead of sleeping, Orville lay awake thinking about the problem. At breakfast he told Wilbur, "While I was awake last night I studied out a new vertical movable rudder to replace the fixed rudder we have used." Wilbur listened carefully to his brother, then, practicing the creative art of invention-extension, advanced Orville's idea. He suggested that they connect the wires that control the wings to those that control the rudder. The idea that one lever could be used to control lateral balance was not only brilliant, it was patentable. Bouncing ideas off each other, the brothers found the last key needed to unlock the problem of heavier-than-air manned flight by applying the principle of force multiplication.

Seamless Teamwork

If there is one word that describes Team Wright, it is this: *seamless*. The Wright brothers were able to operate almost entirely without boundaries or limiting barriers. There was no formal contract or partnership agreement to protect rights and enforce duties. They trusted each other and respected each other's judgment. Although they challenged each other's ideas vigorously, neither felt the need to look over the other's shoulder clandestinely. They worked effortlessly within their own areas of expertise and skill, while keeping the end goal in sight at all times. When Ronald Reagan was president, he kept a sign on his desk that read, "It's amazing what can be accomplished when you don't worry about who gets the credit." No statement could better define Team Wright. Two men, different in so many respects, working seamlessly to accomplish their objectives and goals.

Seamlessness, as it relates to teamwork, is not a spontaneous act of nature. It is the *managed outcome* of vision, purpose, and execution. For Team Wright, that managed outcome is dramatically illustrated in that first flight photo taken by John Daniels on December 17. Although the focus of attention is on Orville and the *Wright Flyer* as it lifts off the launch rail, the eye cannot help but drift to the figure caught in midstride at the side of the machine. Because of the machine's wingspan and slow launch speed, it was necessary for Wilbur to run alongside holding up the wing tip until the flyer gained enough speed to take off on its own. It's appropriate that Wilbur be included in the photo since Orville could not have flown successfully without him.

The Five Equities of Team Wright

The real force multiplier in teamwork is equity. When teams reach an equitable state, the frictions that drag on the team, retarding its progress, are substantially reduced, if not eliminated. The concept of equity, especially as applied to the concept of teamwork, usually focuses on the protection of individual rights. The second and equally important part of the concept—the part that establishes the duties of each person—is often missed. Wilbur and Orville Wright understood this completely. Each brother felt he had not only rights in their relationship, but obligations as well. Team Wright functioned well because the partners paid close attention to the five areas of team equity: trust, effort, profits, power (i.e., information), and honor.

The Equitable Distribution of Trust

Few teammates will ever have to trust each other as much as Wilbur and Orville did. The brothers, in counting on the other to carry out his responsibilities and work, were literally putting their lives in each other's hands. Failure to carry out an assignment, or follow through on a specific detail, could result in a final product that would put their lives in jeopardy. Both brothers knew, however, that they shared two traits in common above all others: a passionate desire to do it right, and complete trust in each other. The respect each of the Wright brothers held for the other is evident throughout their careers. One of the key components of their success, their ability to argue through to the solution of a problem, was the direct result of the trust and respect they had for each other.

One example is the trust the Wright brothers had in each other in their financial dealings. When Wilbur and Orville first went into business together, they opened a joint checking account at the bank. It would be the only account that either brother would have. All funds generated from the operation of the business were deposited into this account. If either brother needed to write a check, he would sign it the same way: *Wright Brothers.* Only a small set of initials (O.W. or W.W.) under the signature would let someone know who had written the check. Neither brother ever questioned the expenditure of the other. This system worked from the beginning until Wilbur's death in 1912.

Those inclined to be more cynical (i.e., less trusting) might point out that the Wright brothers trusted each other because they were related. Blood is thicker than water and all that. I'm sure it had an impact, but being related can have just as many negatives as positives when it comes to trust and respect. The real key to the Wright brothers' ability to trust each other so completely was their shared passion for honesty in all their transactions. In *Grand Eccentrics,* Mark Bernstein notes, "Honesty was the linchpin of Orville's moral universe." It was one constant that Wilbur knew he could count on. It was the reason that Wilbur could share a joint account and never wonder if his brother was taking advantage of him, and vice versa.

The Equitable Distribution of Effort

If the first project undertaken by Team Wright had been the invention of the world's first heavier-than-air flying machine, their efforts might have never gotten off the ground. Like any team, they needed time to process through the normal stages of team development—forming, storming, norming, and performing. The trust they would have in each other needed time to grow and mature. Fortunately for the Wright brothers, concerns over the equitable distribution of work, not to mention profits, were worked out in their first collaborative effort—though it resulted in a heated dispute that required "family arbitration" to resolve.

As a young man, Orville Wright was fascinated by the printing business. When his family moved from Richmond back to Dayton in 1889, he was pleased to discover that Ed Sines, a childhood friend, had acquired a small printing press. Orville helped to upgrade the press, and the firm of Sines & Wright emerged to publish a small neighborhood paper called *The Midget*. Several years later Orville, now well versed in the printing business, decided a larger, more efficient press was needed. When he encountered some obstacles in assembling the press, he hired Wilbur as a "design consultant."

Nothing can break up a team faster than the (real or perceived) inequitable distribution of benefits.

Wilbur didn't just help build the press; he became a permanent part of the team, taking on the responsibilities of editor. When the paper failed, Sines sold his interests to the Wrights and became their first employee.

In *The Bishop's Boys*, Tom Crouch notes that it was during these years as printers and publishers that Wilbur and Orville "worked out the boundaries of their relationship." As Crouch notes, the task was not always an easy one. Although the printing business was originally Orville's idea, he felt at times that Wilbur saw him less as a partner and more as "little brother." Things came to a head in July 1892, when a conflict erupted because Orville thought he was getting the short end of the stick. The case ended up in "family court," the medium Bishop Wright conceived for resolving sibling disputes.

Nothing can break up a team faster than the (real or perceived) inequitable distribution of benefits. Despite the fact that all profits were to be split equally between the brothers, Orville felt that he was carrying the greater burden of work. Frustrated, he demanded that Wilbur renegotiate their agreement. Equally frustrated with his brother, Wilbur submitted the problem to the "Circuit Court of Seven Hawthorn Street." That, of course, was the address of the family residence. Wilbur prepared a mock brief to present his position in the matter. Created as a humorous rendering of a legal document, Wilbur petitioned the "court" to provide an equitable distribution of profits earned, and an apology from Orville. Although the outcome of the "trial" was never recorded, we know the episode must have been a productive one.

The Equitable Distribution of Profits

While demonstrating his flyer in France in 1908, Wilbur decided to compete for the Coupe de Michelin Trophy that had been established by industrialist André Michelin. The trophy, along with 20,000 French francs, would be presented to the person making the longest flight of 1908. Wilbur had already logged a time that doubled that of French flyer Henri Farman, his closest competitor. On December 31, to seal his chances of winning, Wilbur made a flight of two hours and eighteen minutes, three times that of the runner-up.

Following a banquet dinner, with Orville and his sister Katharine in attendance, Wilbur was presented the trophy and cash prize. One of those attending the ceremony was Lieutenant J.T.C. Moore-Barbazon, who shared his recollection of the incident in *Wright Reminiscences*:

> The partnership between the Wright brothers was amusingly and graphically demonstrated at a dinner in Paris where Mr. Michelin, after a suitable speech, presented Wilbur Wright with the prize money they had earned of 20,000 francs. Wilbur expressed his thanks, carefully divided the notes into two packets, and without a word, handed over one packet to his brother, while he put the other in his own pocket.

On the surface it appears that Wilbur was just divvying up the take based on their fifty-fifty partnership. What makes the story interesting is the fact that the brothers, as noted previously, shared a joint checking account. Although Wilbur had split the money between them, both brothers would deposit the funds into their joint account.

I believe that Wilbur was doing more than splitting the proceeds. It would have been uncouth to count out the money in front of others, and highly uncharacteristic of two men of such great modesty. For some reason, I believe, it was necessary for Wilbur to send a message to the audience that theirs—his and Orville's—was a full partnership. Perhaps the adoring crowds had favored one brother over the other. Or perhaps a newspaper article had presented Wilbur as the driving force in the partnership, as it often did. In either case, Wilbur would want to set the record straight. Dividing the money into equal stacks in front of the audience would have surely accomplished that.

The Equitable Distribution of Power (Information)

The first Wright brothers' invention, as far as aviation is concerned, occurred in 1899 when Wilbur and Orville built a five-foot kite to test their wing-warping theory. Wilbur tested the kite for the first time by himself. The mechanism the brothers had designed to warp the wings worked to perfection. Wilbur ran back home to share the information, in great detail, with his brother.

It was a pattern that would characterize their entire working relationship. Wilbur getting information and sharing it with Orville. Orville getting an insight and sharing it with Wilbur. Wilbur once noted that nearly everything that had been done in their lives was the result of "conversations, suggestions, and discussions between us." What one knew, the other knew. By taking a piece of information—an idea, concept, or theory—and bouncing it back and forth between them, the brothers were able to increase their understanding and grasp of the topic. It was force multiplication, the ability to increase the worth of a fact or idea by bouncing it back and forth between them.

Individuals, departments, or divisions that refuse to share information are the biggest stumbling blocks to teamwork. Seeing that information is a source of power or leverage, people withhold it as a card to be played. With the Wright brothers, the free exchange of information was critical. If information was withheld by either of the brothers, it was only until it had been "tumbled about" in the owner's mind in an attempt to find clarity before presenting it. In many organizations, information is hoarded. Let me share an example from my first book, *Management Mess-Ups: 57 Pitfalls You Can Avoid (and Stories of Those Who Didn't)*, of what can happen when information (i.e., power) is freely shared.

Several years ago, I worked with an electronics company that made shared knowledge a key component of its service strategy. Every engineer or salesperson who called on a customer was required to prepare a detailed report of his visit. If, during the course of the visit, a customer problem surfaced, that problem—along with potential solutions—was included in the call report. Most of the time a sketch or two was included as well. These reports were later circulated through every department so that each associate was exposed to the information.

Many companies would regard this process as time-consuming and a poor use of resources. In fact, it had just the opposite effect. I remember one occasion when a customer called during lunch and asked for engineering assistance. The operator switched his call to customer service. When the customer realized he was talking with a service coordinator instead of an engineer, he requested a callback. The service associate then asked if he could reference a particular concern or need. The man replied that he was having a problem with "fretting," a type of corrosion caused by dissimilar materials in a connection. The associate replied, "I might be able to help."

Because the associate had read a call report that not only dealt with this specific problem, but noted the solution, he was able to give the caller the information he needed without necessitating a return call from engineering. The immediate and measurable benefit of the shared knowledge concept in this company was a positive customer experience, but it had the added advantage of empowering and motivating the employee, who felt a vital part of the problem-solving process. Unequal knowledge separates people, compromising their ability to come together as a team.

The Equitable Distribution of Honor

There's a commercial on television that depicts a team just completing an important report. As it comes off the printer, a manager picks it up and "offers" to take it upstairs to the president. But the workers decide to send the information electronically to the president before their boss gets there and takes the glory. When the credit-hogging manager gives the report to the president, he responds curtly, "Already seen it." The ad concludes with the rest of the team members giving each other high fives for having used technology to outwit their boss.

The commercial strikes a chord with viewers because it addresses a common frustration most of us have experienced at work: inequitable distribution of glory. "Troubles arise," Aristotle said, "not over inequalities of property, but inequalities of honor." The best teams have a simple mantra: Share the work, share the glory. More teams have been damaged by the inequitable distribution of honor than of money. That wasn't a problem with the Wright brothers. "They are equal," their father noted, "neither accepting any honor to the exclusion of the other." The best evidence of their commitment to this principle is the fact that any schoolchild who's asked who invented the airplane will reply, "The Wright brothers."

The I/We Index

In January 1920, Orville appeared as a government witness in a lawsuit instituted by the family of aviation pioneer John Montgomery. Montgomery, who had died earlier in a gliding accident, had contended for years that he, not the Wrights, had developed wing-warping. Although the heirs lost their suit, the trial served to generate something of considerable importance: Orville's detailed deposition describing how he and Wilbur had invented the airplane. The account was later published by Dover Publications under the title *How We Invented the Airplane.*

> The force of their partnership was increased more by their differences than by their similarities.

As you read Orville's account, you'll find it difficult to discern much in terms of individual accomplishment. Eight years after Wilbur's untimely death from typhoid fever, Orville goes out of his way to obscure individual contributions. In that 1920 deposition, Orville describes his biggest technical contribution, a movable rear rudder, as follows: "After a good deal of thought the idea occurred to us. . . ." (Not "me," but *us*.) In the deposition, Orville made these other comments as well:

"We gained efficiency in handling the machine . . ."

"We made a number of measurements . . ."

"We made several hundred flights . . ."

"We designed and constructed . . ."

"We decided to build . . ."

"We went to Kitty Hawk . . ."

If the only information a person had about the Wright brothers was what was gleaned from the pages of Orville's deposition, the reader would never know the identity of the brother who failed in his first attempt to fly (Wilbur) or the one who succeeded (Orville). When Bishop Wright was asked which of his sons contributed the most, he replied, "They are equal in their inventions, neither claiming any superiority above the other. . . ." It was the glue that held their team together.

It's been said that the best indicator of a team's development is its I/we ratio. By that standard, Team Wright was extraordinary. How about your team? How often in your meetings and discussions do the words *I* or *we* occur? If your *I*'s exceed your *we*'s, don't be discouraged. Even the Wright brothers had to work on it. When Wilbur wrote his now-famous letter to the Smithsonian Institution in May 1899, he showed it to Orville before sending it. Orville wasn't happy. The source of his displeasure was Wilbur's use of the pronoun "I" throughout his letter. When Orville pointed it out, Wilbur offered to rewrite the letter. Orville, not wanting to waste time or paper, waved Wilbur's offer aside. He was satisfied he had made his point clearly: Theirs would be a partnership of equals.

Getting Ideas Off the Ground

Although there is no shortage of information on the concepts of teams and team building, there are a number of lessons to be learned about team equity from the Wright brothers. When viewed as multiplying factors, the following tips have the ability to increase team effectiveness exponentially.

➜ *Commit to listen . . . really listen.* A critical element in the effectiveness of any organization is its commitment, from top to bottom, to nurture people into becoming extraordinary listeners.

The strength of Team Wright was rooted in the fact that Wilbur and Orville, even in the middle of a heated discussion, *wanted* to hear what the other was saying. The brothers listened intently to each other not just for words, but for meaning.

→ *Take advantage of the "power of difference."* Wilbur and Orville Wright were as different in terms of personality styles as any two people could be. Yet we see that the force of their partnership was increased more by their differences than by their similarities. If this sounds like a pitch for diversity, it is. Organizations with a high degree of diversity tend to also have a high degree of creativity.

→ *Periodically check your team's seams.* Organizations, as well as the departments within them, can inadvertently establish boundaries that inhibit their ability to function as efficiently as needed. These boundaries are often the result of separate agendas, poor communication, physical isolation, or a lack of common vision. Seamlessness is essential to facilitate communication and the free exchange of ideas critical to the problem-solving process.

→ *Share the glory.* Make sure there is an equitable distribution of honor. That is, make sure the final product has the fingerprints of the whole team all over it, and that each team member receives a portion of the glory. The best teams are led by people trying to create stars, not being stars. Remember, any good behavior that goes unacknowledged eventually disappears.

→ *Make everyone accountable.* In a World War II radio speech, Winston Churchill said that although the British people could not guarantee victory, they could guarantee that they deserved victory. Make sure every member of the team has an equitable portion of the assignment, and each member is held accountable for its completion.

→ *Keep information flowing.* Francis Bacon said that information is power. Make sure no one is hoarding information in an effort to increase her power and influence over the team. Sharing information is one of the most powerful ways that someone can let another team member know that he is valued and accepted. Make sure there is an equitable distribution of information.

➡ *Establish bonds of trust.* Recognize that without trust, nothing is possible. The most effective ways to build trust are to maximize listening skills and follow through on commitments. The Wrights kept each other informed regularly. There were never any surprises in their relationship. Avoid a crisis of legitimacy by not making commitments that cannot be met.

➡ *Monitor the I/we ratio.* Periodically check communications (verbal and written) for the words *I* or *me*. Tracking your I/we ratio is the best way yet to make sure your group is maximizing its potential.

One Last Thought

Wilbur's passing on May 30, 1912, thirteen years to the day after he had first written the Smithsonian requesting information on manned flight, concluded the Wright brothers' partnership. His will contained a number of bequests to family members. Most of his estate, however, including rights to the patents, was left to Orville, "who has been associated with me in all the hope and labors of childhood and manhood, and who, I am sure, will use the property in very much the same manner as we would use it together in case we would both survive until old age." *That's* trusting a teammate.

In *Six Great Inventors*, James Crowther gives his readers a bit of extra value by counting the Wright brothers as "one" inventor. In justifying his refusal to draw a distinction between the brothers, Crowther writes:

For the purpose of this book, the Wright brothers have been regarded as one composite inventive personality. Their achievement was the result of mutual inspiration and discussion, and their respective contributions cannot be separated.

Crowther is not the only one who views the brothers this way. The Wright brothers are forever fixed in our minds as one personality because of the extraordinary cohesion of their partnership. It was a collaboration of minds that the world has not seen since.

Note: To view the photos in the Special Collections and Archives section of Wright State University Libraries, visit the website at www.libraries.wright.edu, and follow directions to "The Wright Brothers in Photographs" section.

CHAPTER TEN

SOULS ON FIRE

The most powerful weapon on earth is the human soul on fire.
Ferdinand Foch (1851–1929), French field marshal

A CONCERNED mother sat down and wrote a letter to her son, taking him to task for his inactivity and seeming lack of direction in life. She reminded him that at the age of twenty-two, he needed not only to find a purpose in life, but to work hard to achieve it. "Life means work," she wrote, "and hard work if you mean to succeed." I think it's safe to say that Jennie Churchill's letter to her son had the desired effect. But Winston Churchill wasn't the only youth searching for a purpose in life at the close of the nineteenth century. Four thousand miles away, in a wood-frame house on Hawthorn Street in Dayton, Ohio, another young man was struggling as well.

A Life-Changing Event

Things looked promising for Wilbur Wright his senior year. He had been a good student at Central High School, and he was making plans to attend

Yale Divinity School in the fall, following in his father's footsteps into the ministry. Although not large in stature, he was an all-around athlete who excelled in sports ranging from football to gymnastics, where he was the top athlete in the city on the parallel bars. It wasn't uncommon to find him engaged in a pickup game of some sort around the neighborhood. One day in the spring of 1886, he joined a group of schoolmates on the frozen pond in front of the Soldiers Home outside Dayton for a few rounds of "shinny," an ice-skating game.

The game had been underway for a bit, when Wilbur and another boy found themselves racing to beat each other to the puck. As they neared the puck, the boy swung his bat wildly, missing the puck, but striking Wilbur flush in the face. Wilbur fell to the ground in agony, his mouth a bloody pulp. An army surgeon, observing the injury, rushed to his side to offer aid. All he could do, however, was bandage Wilbur and send him home in great pain. It would take multiple surgeries to repair the damage done to his face and jaw. That was just the beginning.

At a time when friends were making plans for the future, Wilbur was being fitted for false teeth.

At a time when friends were making plans for the future, Wilbur was being fitted for false teeth. Compounding the problem, a few weeks after the injury, he began to experience mysterious heart palpitations and stomach pains that would cause him discomfort the rest of his life. Instead of four years at Yale, Wilbur spent four years at home fighting melancholy and, as his father described it, "tenderly caring for his ailing mother." He put the time to good use, however, reading everything he could put his hands on. In a home that had two well-stocked libraries, that was a lot.

Wilbur Adrift

Three years after Wilbur's injury, Lorin Wright, who had moved to Kansas to seek his own fortune, wrote a letter to his sister Katharine inquiring about his younger brother. "What does Will do?" he asked. "He ought to do something." Lorin went on to inquire patronizingly if Wilbur's duties at home still included those of "cook and chambermaid." His comments may have seemed uncaring, but they reflected the family's growing concern for Wilbur's lack of direction. It was a concern felt by Wilbur himself, who was painfully aware of his situation. His mother had died in July

1889 and, at the age of twenty-two (the same as Winston Churchill), he was without plans for the future. Wilbur lacked purpose in life, something he could put all his passion and energy into. It would take five years for that purpose to arrive, but it would be worth waiting for.

Waiting for the Spark

The Swiss philosopher Henri Frédéric Amiel wrote, "Without passion man is a mere latent force and possibility, like the flint which awaits the shock of the iron before it can give forth its spark." In 1894, Wilbur Wright was a latent force waiting for a purpose to spark his interest. That spark occurred when he picked up a copy of *McClure's Magazine* and saw the photographs of Otto Lilienthal, the "Flying German" who was conducting gliding experiments in the Rhinow Hills outside Berlin. Wilbur carefully read every word, sharing thoughts and ideas on flying with Orville.

Photographs of Lilienthal in flight, carried in hundreds of newspapers, turned the intrepid aviator into a global celebrity. Until his death in 1896, when his glider was upset by a gust of wind and thrown into a stall, Lilienthal had completed more than 2,000 glides. Wilbur had been unusually captivated by Lilienthal's gliding exploits. Perhaps, at some gut level, he felt called on to fill the vacuum created by the German's tragic death. Regardless, he later wrote his father that he was thinking of "making some experiments with a flying machine." "Wilbur was a man," Wright biographer Tom Crouch says, "who established a goal with care, but never lost sight of it." A purpose he would pursue with passion was born that day.

Back Where We Started

We end up back where we started, with the question that won't go away: How were these men able to do what they did? By now, the answer is starting to take shape, but it remains incomplete. Something more is needed to complete the picture. Although many have put forth explanations for the success of the Wright brothers, one who seems, in my opinion, to offer the most intriguing answer is Fred Howard, author of *Wilbur and Orville: A Biography of the Wright Brothers*. Howard believes that Wilbur and Orville Wright were among those "blessed few" who possessed mechanical ability and high intelligence in equal amounts, a fifty-fifty split if you were able to measure such things.

It's not uncommon for people of intelligence to possess little mechanical skill. Bishop Milton Wright, whose analytical skills were considerable, had little mechanical ability. At the same time, it's not uncommon for a person of considerable mechanical ability to lack the mental discipline of a great intellect. Once in a great while, however, someone comes along who happens to possess these gifts in equal measure. Howard calls it a "blessed" event because it occurs so rarely. The odds of its happening to two individuals within the same family are beyond calculating. Even this, however, may not be enough to accomplish something extraordinary. It would take Wilbur and Orville's extraordinary blend of intellect and mechanical aptitude, plus a *passionately held purpose,* to make something great happen.

Had a powerful purpose not presented itself to Wilbur and Orville, their unique blend of intelligence and mechanical aptitude may have remained merely potential. If there's an answer to the question—"Why these guys?"—it may well lie in the unusual concurrence of intellectual and mechanical skills (times two), a unified purpose (build a flying machine), and a passionately held conviction that it was possible to do it. The talent of the Wright brothers would have been wasted without a passionate purpose to activate it. "Genius without direction," Fred Howard wrote, "is genius down the drain."

The Wind Beneath Their Wings

If there was one thing that Wilbur and Orville Wright understood by the winter of 1903, it was the interaction of wind and wing. Years of careful research with their wind tunnel, as well as detailed calculations, had revealed the correct camber to maximize the lifting power of their wings. But there were other forces at work that would provide wind beneath spiritual and emotional wings: Passion and purpose were the force activators that set everything in motion, the energy needed to sustain the brothers through trying times. And trying times were plentiful.

The Wright brothers' second season at Kitty Hawk ended in disappointment and discouragement. After encouraging progress in 1900, the brothers found that their 1901 glider—the largest ever flown up to that time—was in many ways inferior to the previous year's version. One problem after another plagued the men, whose enthusiasm had already been dampened by thunderous storms and swarms of mosquitoes. They were on the verge of packing it in and going home, when they decided to make one last glide.

After a few last-minute adjustments, they hauled their glider up Big Kill Devil Hill to get the height needed for the flight. Wilbur slipped into the hip cradle, then signaled the others he was ready to go. For the first few moments of the flight, the glider behaved itself. Then suddenly it developed what Wilbur called "a mind of its own," darting alarmingly toward the ground. The glide, the last of 1901, concluded with a crash landing that crushed the glider and left Wilbur with a mouthful of sand. It was time to go home.

Although they achieved some success in 1901 (they broke the record for the longest manned flight in a glider), it was a time characterized by a number of events that left them, as Orville noted in his diary, "muddled and confused." The experience of trying to control a machine that fought their efforts to do so left them with a feeling they had not experienced before: fear. Lilienthal's death in an earlier gliding accident was never far from their thoughts. Compounding their concern was the fact that Wilbur's last glide, and its abrupt ending, was strikingly similar to the way Lilienthal had met his demise.

Recalling his discouragement on the train trip back to Dayton that year, Wilbur noted: "When we looked at the time and money which we had expended, and considered the progress made and the distance yet to go, we considered our experiments a failure." Wilbur told Orville that he thought man would one day fly, but that it would not be in their lifetime. Orville summed up their time in Kitty Hawk as "full of problems" and "the most miserable experience I have ever passed through." Their departure from Kitty Hawk in August 1901 was engulfed in a cloud of confusion and disappointment. Both men, at the gut level, thought their work on the flying problem was over.

A Measure of Desire

There's an old proverb that says, "Dwell not upon thy weariness, thy strength shall be according to the measure of thy desire." Apparently, Wilbur and Orville didn't give their weariness much thought. The strength of their desire returned full measure, and they were back in Kitty Hawk the following August. This time, they moved their camp four miles west to be closer to the big dunes at Kill Devil Hills needed to launch their glider.

The discouragement of 1901 now in their rearview mirror, they resumed work with a fire and intensity not shown before. During the 1902 season, Wilbur and Orville made hundreds of test glides on Big Kill Devil Hill. Time after time, despite weariness and fatigue, they hauled their glider up the dune to get one last glide in before calling it quits. Then they'd do another one anyway. Some days they'd get their glider to the top of the hill only to discover that a capricious wind had disappeared. What made them keep going?

> Time after time they hauled their glider up the dune to get "one last glide" in before calling it quits.

Unplowed Fields

During an undergraduate course in physics, I remember being taught the concepts of potential and kinetic energy. Potential energy is the energy a mass has simply because of its relationship to something else. Unlike kinetic energy, which represents everything already in motion, potential energy remains unrealized until something happens to spur it on. It's like an unplowed field. The potential is there for a bountiful harvest, but not without first planting seed. In the winter of 1901, Wilbur and Orville had no small amount of potential (creative) energy. But it was desperately in need of a force to set it in motion. As the brothers continued their discussions at work and after dinner in the evenings, that force began to surface. The force that changed their potential energy into kinetic energy, in the creative sense, can be summed up in three words: passion, purpose, and vision.

Afflicted with Belief

When Wilbur wrote to the Smithsonian Institution in 1899 to request information on aviation, he was directed to a book written by Octave Chanute called *Progress in Flying Machines*. After he and Orville had read the book, Wilbur wrote Chanute to request additional information and advice. In his letter he said, "I'm afflicted with the belief that man will fly, and I'm afraid it will one day cost me all my money if not my life." On the surface, the writing may have seemed a bit overdramatic, but it reflected the true passion of its writer.

Well-read and highly literate, Wilbur had a marvelous vocabulary at his disposal to describe his feelings. He might have said he was enamored and fascinated with, or even curious about, heavier-than-air flight. *Affliction,* however, was the word that described the grip that flying had taken of his soul. It was also a word with which he had already had a good bit of experience. With the recollection of difficult times anchored in his memory, I believe Wilbur knew exactly what he was trying to convey when he wrote to Chanute. Wilbur's desire to conquer the air was a malady just as real and potent as the pain he still experienced from his skating accident years earlier.

Passionate Statements

Orville, blessed with the gift of fantasy, had a well-defined mental picture of future success. After making his historic first flight, a reporter asked him if he was excited the night before the event. Orville responded that he was not. The reporter, surprised at his answer, asked why not. Orville said he had already flown so many times in his mind that when it finally occurred, it was just another flight! His vision was so intense that it served as a sort of "cosmic magnet" pulling him toward destiny. For Orville, **Orville's vision was so intense that it served as a sort of "cosmic magnet" pulling him toward destiny.** the actual flight was almost anticlimactic. He had lived with that vision of success for so long that it had become reality in his mind. December 17, 1903, marked just another flight to Orville.

Both quotes—Wilbur's on affliction and Orville's on vision—hang on the wall in my office as constant reminders of two critical ingredients needed to make ideas soar. When people look for reasons why the Wright brothers were successful in solving the problem of heavier-than-air controlled flight, these two statements should not be overlooked. The mechanical and technical skills of the Wrights were many. They were meticulous, methodical, and detailed. They were clear, crisp thinkers able to thoroughly evaluate and analyze every problem. They even followed a set of problem-solving principles. What powered their effort, however, the thing that drove them from Dayton to the dunes of Kill Devil Hills, was passionate vision.

Louis-Pierre Mouillard, an early flying-machine pioneer, knew exactly how the Wright brothers felt. In his book *Empire of the Air,* he wrote:

> If there be a domineering, tyrant thought it is the conception that the problem of flight may be solved by man. When once this idea has invaded the brain it possesses it exclusively. It is then a haunting thought, a walking nightmare, impossible to cast off. If now we consider the pitying contempt with which such a line of research is appreciated, we may somewhat conceive the unhappy lot of the poor investigator whose soul is thus possessed.

Without passion and vision, the wind beneath their wings, the Wright brothers might never have driven their ideas to a successful conclusion. Like many before them, they might have chosen to let someone else attack the impossible. Like Mouillard, however, their souls were possessed, and the only option was to go forward.

Many Had Dreamed . . .

Many men had dreamed of flying, but few had seen the possibility as clearly as Orville or pursued it with as much intensity as Wilbur. What's your affliction? What's your vision? What do you believe in so strongly that you are willing to risk all your money, if not your life? It's a question I've asked myself on many occasions. Outside of my spiritual convictions, I'm usually hard-pressed to identify anything I could put in the "afflicted" category. I'm anxious to do so, because that would be the one thing I would most likely achieve. If we believe in something strongly enough, we find a way to make it happen. It worked for the Wright brothers, and it will work for us.

Force Activators

It's important to remember that vision and passion, as presented here, are not in themselves problem-solving principles. They are, however, the force that energizes them. Without the energy that passion brings, the principle of constructive conflict (or what I call *forging*) becomes a toothless tiger. Without the intensity of strongly held beliefs, the principle of forever learning (through *relentless preparation*) becomes another failed resolution. The benefits of being passionate about your work, your purpose, or your beliefs provide the lift needed to get your ideas, products, or programs off the ground and in the air. Here are a few examples.

How Passion for Their Purpose Benefited Wilbur and Orville

- *It drove them past obstacles.* The Wright brothers' gliding experiments in 1901 would have led most people to quit. They left Kitty Hawk that year "muddled and confused," with little confidence they would ever build another glider. Few worthwhile endeavors are free of frustration. Delays, diversions, and discouragement will certainly present themselves at one point or another. The strength of your belief in your purpose, however, can power you through these difficulties. The Wright brothers returned to Kitty Hawk because, as biographer Fred Kelly notes, their passion had been "too much aroused for them to quit."

- *It gave them the power to ignore negative feedback.* I can't imagine how many people came into the Wright brothers' bicycle shop and offered thoughts about their flying machine. "If God had meant for man to fly, He would have given him wings!" I bet they never tired of hearing that one. Despite the ridicule—because that's what it was—the brothers were able to continue. They were lifted up by their strongly held belief that man would one day fly, and that they would be the first to do it.

- *It kept them focused on their objective, the source of their passion.* Their flying machine was always in their line of vision, a constant reminder of what the overall goal was. Wilbur and Orville broke the problem into smaller, more manageable components in order to solve it, but the ultimate objective was always there. On more than a few occasions, when the brothers reached an impasse in their work, they may have thought about putting the whole thing on the back burner for later consideration. Their passion kept their objective front and center.

- *It helped to energize them mentally, physically, and emotionally.* Orville's enthusiasm overflowed in 1903 when the Wright brothers were working on their wind tunnel. Orville recalled those days as difficult but energizing. In two months' time, they made thousands of measurements, then plugged the numbers into formulas for calculating lift and drag. Reminiscing about their work years later, Orville recalled that "Wilbur and I could hardly wait for morning to come to get at something that interested us. That's happiness!" It's also passion. Thoughts of our work should be among our happiest.

➻ *It converted interest into action.* Much is made of the toy helicopter Bishop Wright gave his sons, because it was the spark that would later ignite their simmering interest in flying. It's worth remembering that thousands of American children had Pénaud helicopters, but only two of them invented a flying machine. A passion for purpose converted interest into action for Wilbur and Orville. Without it, their interest in flying would have just been a passing phase.

➻ *It kept them looking forward.* I like to call it "rearview mirror" thinking, this habit we all have of dwelling on the past, looking at all the mistakes we've piled up behind us. Passion for purpose kept the Wright brothers pressing on to what lay ahead. They were always moving forward, thinking of the next thing to do. As Charlie Taylor, the brothers' mechanic, liked to say: "They didn't waste much time worrying about the past." Passion for purpose is, as my daughter likes to say, all about moving forward.

➻ *It was contagious.* Wilbur caught the flying fever from Lilienthal and Mouillard. Initially, Orville did not share his brother's enthusiasm, but Wilbur's increasingly passionate interest was contagious. As Wilbur continued to talk about the problem of manned flight, sharing with his brother articles, ideas, books, and theories, Orville found himself drawn into the challenge. Soon, he was just as committed as Wilbur was to solving the problem.

➻ *It changed their perspective on problems.* Another Dayton visionary and inventor, Charles Kettering, once told a staff member, "Don't bring me anything but trouble . . . good news weakens me!" A passionate purpose changes your perspective about difficulties.

They cease to exist as troubles and become opportunities instead. In a letter to their friend and fellow experimenter George Spratt, Orville wrote, "Isn't it wonderful that all these secrets have been preserved for so many years just so that we could discover them." A passionate purpose changed forever how Wilbur and Orville viewed problems.

➤ *It quenched their thirst.* A life lived in the pursuit of goals for which you have only mediocre interest is like wandering for years in an arid desert. Passion restores the soul, sets it on fire, then quenches its thirst. In conquering the December skies of Kill Devil Hills, Wilbur and Orville drank deeply of the only thing that quenches an inventor's thirst—success.

Wilbur and Orville often played off each other. When one brother became frustrated or discouraged, the other reenergized him with his enthusiasm and passion. As long as their souls remained on fire, they knew they could get where they were going.

Learning to Soar

Just as Wilbur was better because of Orville (and vice versa), so are vision and passion enhanced when blended together. When I was a young man, my father used to tell me: "You can have whatever you want if you're willing to do the necessary work." He was partly right. You can have whatever you want, if you can see it clearly, believe in it passionately, and do the necessary work. Here are a few tips for making that happen.

➤ *Have a well-defined vision.* There's a good deal of evidence that we tend to achieve what we can most clearly see. Don't be satisfied with moderate interests. Look for that which sets your soul afire, then figure out ways to keep that vision in front of your eyes.

➤ *Picture the desired outcome with intense imagination.* In a letter from Paris, Wilbur told his father, "My imagination pictures things more vividly than my eyes." Both Wilbur and Orville had the ability to "see" the end goal—to visualize it actually happening. As a result, mental, physical, and emotional energies were released to bring that vision into being.

➡ *Remember that great ideas need landing gear, as well as wings.* Though it's important to have "wind under your wings," knowing where you intend to land is equally important. It's wise to make present decisions with the end objective firmly in mind. Wilbur and Orville made every decision based on one criterion: Does it take us closer to our goal (heavier-than-air, powered and controlled flight)?

➡ *Convert passion into meaningful steps.* Contrary to popular opinion, passion is not without form and structure. Wilbur was very focused: He planned in advance his next steps. He knew where he was going, and he had the doggedness to pursue the steps that would take him there. There is considerable passion in reason.

➡ *Identify your ruling passion.* Most of us have one passion that rises above all others. To identify it, and isolate it from all the other interests that clamor for attention, try working backward. Imagine that your life has come to a conclusion and you'll be remembered for one thing only. What, in your heart of hearts, would you want that to be?

➡ *Fan the flames.* At times in our lives, the flames of our passion may resemble dying embers. Fanning the flames of our passion will rekindle not only our interest, but our commitment. After spending a great deal of time on this book, I found myself growing weary of it. A trip to Kitty Hawk, where I was able to once again walk in the footsteps of the Wright brothers, quickly restored my passion for gleaning present-day advice from the lives of these men.

➡ *Keep passion in check.* Strongly held, even passionate beliefs often need to be held in check. When Wilbur began his experiments in Kitty Hawk in 1900, he was anxious to fly. Although willing to take risks, he made sure they were highly calculated. In a letter to his father, Wilbur wrote: "The man who wishes to keep at the problem long enough to really learn something positively must not take dangerous risks. Carelessness and overconfidence are usually more dangerous than deliberately accepted risks."

Passion Fuels Effort

One of the more passionate artists in history was Michelangelo, whose true love was sculpting. Often, though, he needed to accept painting commissions to earn a living. When he received payment, the first thing he did was go to the quarry to buy another block of stone for his chisel. Michelangelo would grow sullen and anxious if his painting kept him away from sculpting for long. He would begin to suffer what he called "marble fever" until he could once more put hammer and chisel to stone. For Wilbur and Orville, the feeling was no less intense. In the summer months that kept them away from the sandy beaches and dunes of Kill Devil Hills, the brothers pined for the opportunity to escape their bicycle business and soar once more over windswept dunes. It was not a consuming fever, but a fever that kept alive a burning desire to complete their purpose.

For Wilbur and Orville, the effort needed—emotionally as well as physically—would be enormous. It wasn't uncommon for the men to return from the Outer Banks weighing a few pounds less than when they left. Repeatedly hauling their gliders up Big Kill Devil Hill took its toll. In *Visions of a Flying Machine,* Peter Jakab writes, "One can only attain a true sense of the energy expended in this activity by actually carrying such a machine up a hundred-foot ridge of sand several dozen times in the afternoon." When I was there during the month of October, I decided to walk up and down the hill several times to see just how grueling a workout it was. After my fourth trip, I decided to quit. I was totally exhausted, and the only weight I carried was my Pentax camera.

In the final analysis, we are all evaluated by the quality of our effort. It's the mark we place on our work; it shows the world how much we believe in what we are doing. The effort we make in accomplishing something is the measure of the passion we have for it. Following his mother's advice, Winston Churchill pursued his goals with a tireless effort. His mother's words may have been in his ears when he spoke to the British people during the German bombing of London in 1940–1941. In a memorable address, Churchill told his countrymen that although they could not guarantee victory, they could guarantee that they deserved it. "Deserve Victory" became a rallying cry to the British people. The extra effort put forth may have been just enough to defeat the Germans. Or, in the case of Wilbur and Orville Wright, to conquer the wind.

One Last Thought

On December 17, 1948, forty-five years after it made the world's first heavier-than-air powered flight, the original *Wright Flyer* was returned to the United States. Decades of contention with the Smithsonian Institution finally resolved, the Wright brothers' invention was enshrined in its rightful place of honor. During comments made on behalf of the estate of Orville Wright, a nephew, Milton Wright, shared his lack of surprise upon learning for the first time that his uncles had flown. "I was not impressed by the fact that they had flown," he said in his presentation speech, "because, from conversations I had overheard, I knew they had figured out how to do it, and things they figured out usually worked."

It's been said that our actions tend to follow our most habitual thoughts. Almost from the beginning, before they had cut the first piece of wood or sewn the first piece of fabric for their flying machine, the Wright brothers' most habitual thought was that they could succeed at flying. In May 1900 Wilbur wrote to Octave Chanute, "It is my belief that flight is possible." That belief powered the brothers into the air just as much as the little twelve-horsepower motor on their *Wright Flyer* did.

In his remarks to the Smithsonian, Milton Wright described his famous uncles as "very normal young men who had an idea and saw a problem and set about to solve that problem." I like his comment, because it takes the spotlight off the brothers and places it on the action they took. They set about to solve the problem. By placing our attention on the process and not the men, we gain both a clearer understanding of the men, and an understanding of the principles that comprise *The Wright Way* of solving problems. Applying these principles to your business challenges (e.g., to generate ideas, products, projects, and strategies) will not only get your company off the ground, but will make it soar!

LIVES OF CONSEQUENCE

ON MARCH 23, 1903, Wilbur and Orville Wright petitioned the United States government for a patent on their flying machine. Their request was not based on the powered flyer of 1903, but on their 1902 glider. Feeling there was nothing unusual about their motor, the brothers based their request on the uniqueness of their wing-warping system of control, complete with movable rudder. The patent office, which had by that time received more than 50,000 requests for flying machine patents, rejected the Wright brothers' petition. The letter accompanying their returned application described their drawing and description as "indefinite, inadequate, and vague."

The brothers reworked their application, adding more detail in an effort to provide greater clarity. This time, Wilbur even enclosed an inner tube box so the examiner could see the wing-warping principle as Wilbur had first conceived it. The request was again rejected. This time, though, it was sent back with a useful suggestion: Get a lawyer. Especially one who specializes in patent law. The brothers acted on the patent examiner's advice and once again submitted an application for approval. It would be three years before the brothers would hear a disposition of their request.

Before receiving their patent, the Wright brothers all but disappeared from the aviation scene. Legitimately concerned that someone might try and steal their invention, the brothers did not fly in public again for three years after Kill Devil Hills. Finally, on May 22, 1906, the United States government granted Wilbur and Orville Wright patent number 821,393 for a "new and useful improvement in Flying Machines." Competitors now had three choices: Sign a license agreement, pay royalties, or stay grounded. For all intents and purposes, Wilbur and Orville Wright now controlled the skies. Even after their patent was issued, however, the brothers remained cautious. A number of bitter patent fights followed, causing the brothers to divert valuable research time to legal matters. The brunt of the fight fell on Wilbur, who was the more articulate and made the better witness in the hearings that ensued.

The legal battles, which required a great deal of travel and court time, took their toll on Wilbur. While testifying at a hearing in Boston in the spring of 1912, he became ill. At first he thought he had a case of food poisoning, but by the time he arrived back in Dayton he had a raging fever. Examined by local doctors, Wilbur was diagnosed with the one disease the family dreaded most: typhoid fever. Like his brother, who had contracted it sixteen years earlier, Wilbur courageously battled the disease for weeks. Emotionally and physically exhausted by legal battles and difficulties, however, Wilbur did not have the strength needed to recover. On May 30, 1912, Bishop Milton Wright made the following entry into his diary:

> This morning at 3:15, Wilbur passed away, aged 45 years, 1 month, 14 days. A short life, full of consequences. An unfailing intellect, imperturbable temper, great self-reliance and as great modesty, seeing the right clearly, pursuing it steadily, he lived and died.

Power to Control the Skies

In his will, Wilbur Wright left his rights to their flying machine patents to his brother. Orville now controlled one of the most important patents in history. The patent, valid through 1917, was so far-reaching that virtually anyone who wanted to build a flying machine would have to pay a licensing fee to Orville's company. Had Orville had a stomach for industry and ruthless business dealings, his patent could have generated immeasurable wealth. He could have become a billionaire and joined the Rockefellers, Astors, and Morgans of the world.

But Orville was tired. With the passing of his brother, the light had gone out of his life. Orville would never be the same, overcome for the rest of his life with what his niece, Ivonette Wright Miller, called a "spirit of loneliness." He sold the Wright Company to investors and spent the rest of his life doing what he loved best: tinkering in his shop. He died on January 30, 1948, following his second heart attack in two months. He survived his brother by thirty-six years and lived to see the advent of jet-powered aircraft.

A Problem-Solving Legacy

The story of Wilbur and Orville Wright is more than the story of flight. It's the story of two men who, through the systematic application of problem-solving principles, managed to do what no one else had been able to do. The importance of the Wright brothers' flying machine to the world is beyond dispute. A contribution of nearly equal value, however, remains to be discovered by businesses facing challenges nearly as daunting as those faced by Wilbur and Orville. By applying the principles the Wright brothers used to today's business challenges, companies will not only get their ideas off the ground, they will make them soar!

The number 821,393 is on the front of my computer, placed there to remind me that no problem is ever truly impossible to solve. It may take time, it may take effort, and it may take careful consideration. But it can be solved. Edward Deeds, another noted Daytonian, said: "Our lives and the lives of our children, and our children's children, depend upon our breadth of vision, unity of purpose, and courage to execute." Perhaps more than anything else, the courage to execute is the thing most needed to solve a problem. Otto Lilienthal, who gave his life advancing the science of flight, had it. Samuel Langley, who sacrificed his reputation and career in pursuit of flight, had it. Wilbur and Orville Wright, afflicted with the belief that man could fly, had it.

The most fitting epilogue to the Wright story, one no writer can improve upon, was offered by John Daniels, the surfman from the Kill Devil Hills Lifesaving Station who took the photograph of Orville's triumphant moment. *Twelve Seconds to the Moon* recounts Daniels's thoughts about December 17, 1903:

> I like to think about that first airplane the way it sailed off into the air at Kill Devil Hills that morning, as pretty as any bird you ever laid eyes on. I don't think I ever saw a prettier sight in my life. Its wings and uprights were braced with new and shiny copper piano wires. The sun was shining bright that morning, and the wires just blazed in the sunlight like gold. The machine looked like some big, graceful golden bird sailing off into the wind. I think it made us all feel kind of meek and prayerful like. It might have been a circus for some folks, but it wasn't any circus for those of us who lived close to those Wright boys during all the months until we were as much wrapped up in the fate of the thing as they were. It wasn't luck that made them fly; it was hard work and hard common sense; they put their whole heart and soul and all of their energy into an idea and they had the faith. Good Lord, I'm-a-wondering what all of us could do if we had the faith in our ideas and put all of our heart and mind and energy into them like those Wright boys did.

Side-by-Side at Last

On May 25, 1910, Wilbur and Orville accompanied their father to Huffman Prairie, where the eighty-two-year-old cleric would fly for the first time with Orville. Before that, however, the brothers requested his permission—for posterity's sake—to fly together. For two men who had shared so much, who had worked side-by-side for so many years in solving the problem of heavier-than-air flight, there was one thing they had not shared. They had never flown together. It was a promise Wilbur and Orville had made to their father when they began their experiments in

1900, and they always kept their word. Today, however, the Bishop relented and gave his consent.

As Wilbur and Orville took their places beside each other in their Model B *Wright Flyer*, the two aviators—history's first—began to taxi across the bumpy field. Slowly, their flyer lifted off the ground into the dimming light of the early summer evening. As the brothers made a slow turn and passed over their father, they exchanged a wave. One can't help but wonder what the conversation of the two men might have been. Charlie Taylor, the Wright brothers' chief mechanic, may have had the answer. "They were always thinking of the next thing to do," Taylor recalled. "They didn't waste much time worrying about the past." The masters of the problem had conquered the skies and were no doubt setting their sights on new horizons.

APPENDICES

IN A BOOK of this nature, it is sometimes difficult to put individuals and events in proper sequence. To assist the reader who wants to properly frame the story, I have included some information that should prove useful. The first is a chronology, a listing of significant dates and events in the Wright brothers' story (life and work). That's followed by short biographies of aviation pioneers and other key individuals mentioned in the book. It was less disruptive to the storytelling to put the profiles of this cast of characters in this separate section, rather than to try and weave the story of each person into the chapters themselves.

I've also provided a bibliography and recommended reading list for those wishing to take their knowledge of the subject to another level. Lastly, I've included a modest listing of aviation terms used in the book, as well as a definition of each. Since I'm neither a pilot nor an aviation authority, I found these terms helpful in understanding what the Wright brothers were doing and why. It's my hope that these appendices will assist the reader in getting the most out of *The Wright Way*.

Chronology of Important Events

1485   Leonardo da Vinci sketches detailed plans for a flying machine.

1859   Bishop Milton Wright marries Susan Catherine Koerner.

1861   Reuchlin Wright is born in Grant County, Indiana.

1862   Lorin Wright is born in Dublin County, Indiana.

1867   Wilbur Wright is born on April 16 on a small farm near Millville, Indiana.

1868   Wright family moves to 7 Hawthorn Street in Dayton, Ohio.

1871   Orville Wright is born on August 19 at home on Hawthorn Street.

1874   Katharine Wright is born on August 19 at home on Hawthorn Street.

1878   Wright family moves to Cedar Rapids, Iowa and leases the Hawthorn Street house.

1878   Milton Wright returns from a trip with a toy helicopter for his sons.

1881   Wright family moves to Richmond, Indiana.

1884   Wright family returns to Dayton.

1885   Wright family moves back to house at 7 Hawthorn Street.

1886   Wilbur is seriously injured in a game of "shinny" (a form of hockey).

1886   Orville Wright and Ed Sines form company, Sines & Wright-Job Printers.

1888   Orville builds printing press; Wilbur "consults" on the project.

1889   Wright brothers establish the *West Side News*, a weekly newspaper, in March (their first collaboration).

1889   Susan Wright dies on July 4.

1890   Wright brothers establish *The Evening Item*, a daily newspaper (Wilbur editor, Orville publisher).

1890   Wright & Wright-Job Printers is formed (their first official business) after *Evening Item* fails.

1892   The "safety" bicycle craze reaches Dayton.

1892   The Wright Cycle Exchange is established at 1005 West Third Street in Dayton.

1893   Business moves to 1034 West Third Street and is renamed the Wright Cycle Company.

1894   Wright brothers read article in *McClure's Magazine* on Otto Lilienthal and flying.

1895   Wright brothers move their growing bicycle business to 22 South Williams Street.

1896   Orville contracts typhoid fever in September, beginning six-week bout with illness.

1896   Otto Lilienthal dies on August 10 in gliding accident outside Berlin.

1897   Business moves to 1127 West Third Street, where the *Wright Flyer* is developed.

1899   Wilbur writes letter to the Smithsonian Institution on May 30, requesting reading material on aeronautics.

1899   Wright brothers build a steerable biplane kite to test wing-warping theory.

1900   Wilbur writes letter to Octave Chanute on May 13, requesting guidance on research efforts.

1900   Wright brothers build their first man-carrying glider.

1900   Wilbur and Orville take their glider to Kitty Hawk, North Carolina, for flight tests (September 12 to October 23).

1901   Wilbur and Orville return to Kill Devil Hills with new glider (July 11 to August 22).

1901   Wilbur speaks to the Western Society of Engineers in Chicago on September 18.

1901   Wilbur and Orville build wind tunnel and test designs from October to December.

1902   Wilbur and Orville complete construction of a new glider based on wind tunnel tests.

1902   Wilbur and Orville return to Kill Devil Hills to test new glider (August 25 to October 28).

1903   Wilbur and Orville return to Kill Devil Hills with powered flyer (September 23 to December 22).

1903   Wright brothers file for patent based on control system of their 1902 glider.

1903   Wilbur fails in first attempt to fly the *Wright Flyer* on December 14.

1903   Orville succeeds in second attempt to fly the *Wright Flyer* on December 17.

1904   Wilbur and Orville move experiments to Huffman Prairie near Dayton.

1905 First practical flying machine, the *Wright Flyer III,* is developed at Huffman Prairie.

1906 On May 22, the U.S. Patent Office grants basic Wright patent, No. 821,393.

1908 Wrights make first public exhibition flights in Le Mans, France.

1908 Orville crashes flyer during tests, suffering severe injuries; passenger is killed.

1909 The Wright Company is incorporated with Wilbur as president and Orville vice president.

1910 Wilbur and Orville make their only flight together on May 25 at Huffman Prairie.

1912 Wilbur dies at the age of 45 from typhoid fever on May 30 in Dayton.

1914 Wright family builds a new home (Hawthorn Hill) in Oakwood, a Dayton suburb.

1917 Bishop Milton Wright dies at the age of 89.

1918 Orville makes his final flight as a pilot on May 13.

1948 Orville dies at home on January 30, following a stroke, at the age of 77.

2003 Centennial celebration of world's first heavier-than-air, powered and controlled flight.

*   *   *

Short Biographies of Aviation Pioneers and Experimenters

Ader, Clément (1844–1925) Known as the "Father of French Aviation," Ader was a self-taught engineer whose early work was in the field of communications. A pioneer in the development of the telephone, Ader was responsible for creating the microphone and public address system. In 1872, he turned his attention to the problem of heavier-than-air flight. Over the next twenty-five years, he would build three flying machines, the *Éole, Avion II,* and *Avion III.* Although Ader made many contributions to manned flight, his claims of having successfully flown for a distance of 900 feet have been discarded. Witnesses of the flight described it as full of "short hops," with one of three wheels always on the ground.

Cayley, George (1773–1857) Often called the "father of flight" because of his breakthrough research at the beginning of the nineteenth century, Cayley was the first true scientific aerial investigator. A Yorkshire baronet, Cayley was the first to understand the underlying principles of flight and refute the ornithopter (i.e., wing flapping) propulsion theory prevalent at the time. Cayley not only discovered that a curved lifting surface (i.e., a wing) would generate more lift than a flat one, he applied that knowledge in building the first successful man-carrying glider. In 1853, Cayley's three-wing glider, carrying his gardener, traveled over 900 feet before crash landing. Cayley's research was recorded in a three-part monograph, "On Aerial Navigation," published in 1810 in *Nicholson's Journal of Natural Philosophy*. Arguably one of the most important papers written in the quest to invent the airplane, Cayley correctly defined lift, propulsion, and control as the three key elements of heavier-than-air flight. Using applied science, Cayley was the first to correctly frame the heavier-than-air flying problem as "making a surface support a given weight by the application of power to the resistance of air." Cayley was never able to build the machine itself.

Chanute, Octave (1832–1910) When Wilbur Wright wrote the Smithsonian Institution in 1899 requesting information on aeronautics, one of the recommendations he received was Octave Chanute's *Progress in Flying Machines*. The book would not only become a major resource for the Wright brothers, it would lead to an exchange of correspondence that would last a decade, providing later historians with invaluable insights into the work of the two brothers. Chanute, a highly acclaimed civil engineer, had dedicated his retirement years to seeking out and organizing all known aeronautical information to date for his book. His interest roused in the process, Chanute began gliding experiments of his own at Indiana Dunes in 1896. Chanute was inducted into the National Aviation Hall of Fame in 1963 for his role as a collector and disseminator of aeronautical information. His greatest contribution, however, may have been as a facilitator and encourager of the Wright brothers in their quest to solve the problem of flight.

Curtiss, Glenn (1878–1930) Known in aviation circles as the "father of naval aviation," Curtiss got his start in business building engines for bicycles and motorcycles. The lightweight engines he developed were soon in demand by makers of dirigibles. In many respects, Curtiss picked up where the Wright brothers left off in terms of aviation development. He developed the flying boat and was responsible for the first takeoff and landing from the deck of a ship at sea. Curtiss is principally remembered, however, for being a thorn in the side of the Wright brothers for years because of his legal battles with them over their patent rights. Orville would attribute Wilbur's untimely death to Curtiss's attempts to steal the Wright brothers' patents.

Gibbs-Smith, Sir Charles H. (1909–1981) Gibbs-Smith is one of the most important aviation historians. Gibbs-Smith's *The Invention of the Aeroplane* gives an excellent year-by-year, craft-by-craft account of the airplane between 1799 and 1909. Gibbs-Smith divided aerial pioneers into two groups: "chauffeurs" and "airmen." He chose the name "chauffeur" for the first group because of their belief that, once in the air, planes could be piloted much as one drives a car. Chauffeurs focused on propulsion. "Airmen" were those who focused primarily on gliding as a means of working out the problems of lift and control.

Langley, Samuel Pierpont (1834–1906) In the fall of 1903, three men were on the verge of claiming history's first sustained flight of a heavier-than-air, man-carrying flying machine: Wilbur and Orville Wright, and Samuel Pierpont Langley. A highly respected physicist and astronomer, Langley was the head of the Smithsonian Institution. He had begun experimenting with model flying machines in 1887, building rubber-band-powered models that flew 80–100 feet. Later, he would develop steam-powered models that would fly thousands of feet before running out of fuel. In August 1903, he constructed a one-quarter-size model of a proposed flyer. Called an *Aerodrome*, Langley's model flew a distance of 1,000 feet. Convinced he now had the answer to flight in hand, Langley built a full-size flying machine, the *Great Aerodrome*, in October 1903. On October 7, Charles Manly, inventor of the internal combustion engine that powered it, attempted to fly Langley's machine. It collapsed on takeoff. A second attempt on December 9 experienced similar results. A little more than a week later, Wilbur and Orville Wright claimed "first flight" honors. Mercilessly derided and ridiculed by the press, Langley died a broken and bitter man in 1906, his greatest contribution to aviation two 30-pound models flown in 1896.

Lilienthal, Otto (1848–1896) Few individuals made as significant, if not courageous, contributions to the science of flight as Otto Lilienthal. A gifted German mathematician and mechanical engineer, Lilienthal thought the solution to the problem of heavier-than-air flight lay partly in calculation, partly in experimentation. For years, he studied all known data on flight, then in just five years made more than 2,000 flights in eighteen different glider models. He was the first person to make successful, reproducible glides. Photographs of the "intrepid birdman," seen in magazines and newspapers all over the world, served to legitimize the efforts of those attacking the heavier-than-air flying problem. On August 8, 1896, Lilienthal was critically injured in a gliding attempt. It's said that moments before dying on August 10, Lilienthal uttered, "Sacrifices must be made." Lilienthal's death is credited by the Wright brothers as a key event that ignited their interest in the flying problem.

Maxim, Hiram Stevens (1840–1916) One of the more interesting pioneers in early aviation was Hiram Maxim, inventor of the Maxim machine gun. Born in Maine, Maxim moved to England in 1881, where he used a considerable portion of his wealth in an attempt to solve the heavier-than-air flying problem. In 1893, Maxim constructed his famous Biplane Test-Rig at Baldwyns Park, England. The machine, weighing nearly 7,000 pounds, was powered by two enormous steam engines, each capable of generating over 180 horsepower. The engines turned two "pusher"-style propellers measuring 17.5 feet in diameter. A proponent of the "chauffeur," school of thought, Maxim believed anything could be made to fly with enough power. Maxim did succeed in getting his Biplane Test-Rig, carrying himself and three other men, off the ground in 1894. With 10,000 pounds of force generated, however, the machine caromed out of control, never reaching an altitude of much more than two or three feet. Maxim built a biplane in 1910, but he was never successful in getting it to fly.

Montgomery, John (1858–1911) Although many are credited with making glides prior to 1900, John Montgomery holds the honor of making the world's first "controlled flight" in a heavier-than-air craft in 1883. Montgomery's glide, which took place near San Diego and covered 600 feet, demonstrated his grasp of aerodynamic principles gained from years of study and independent research. His 1883 glider was the first to incorporate flight controls and a shaped airfoil. Montgomery continued to conduct research on manned flight, and his papers were included in Octave Chanute's book *Progress in Flying Machines*, which was released in 1894. In October 1911, while making a glide, Montgomery was jostled by a gust of wind, causing his head to strike a stove bolt on his glider. He died shortly thereafter. Montgomery's heirs brought a patent infringement suit against the Wright-Martin Aircraft Company, holder of the Wright patents, but dropped the suit when it became apparent there was no basis for the claim.

Pénaud, Alphonse (1850–1880) Alphonse Pénaud, often referred to as the "father of flying models," had a short but eventful life. The son of a French admiral, he had planned a naval career. When a crippling illness ended that dream, he quickly directed his considerable skills toward the problem of manned flight. He was the first person to successfully build and fly heavier-than-air model flying machines. The Pénaud *Planophore*, which used a rubber-band-powered "pusher," was flown in Paris in 1871. Although just a model, it was the first truly stable airplane in history. Later Pénaud models would feature such innovations as twin propellers, retractable landing gear, a unified elevator, and rudder control. Pénaud published numerous articles concerning airflow, resistance, and the characteristics of gliding flight. Depressed over his inability to raise the funds needed to convert his models into full-size machines, Pénaud took his life in 1880. Ironically, the Wright brothers would credit the Pénaud toy helicopter, which they had received as a gift from their father, as one of the earliest influences sparking their interest in manned flight.

Pilcher, Percy Sinclair (1867–1899) After six years in the Royal Navy and several more as an engineer, Percy Pilcher turned his interest to flying. One of the few British participants to try his hand at solving the flying problem, Pilcher built his first glider—the "Bat"—in early 1895. Later that year he met with German engineer Otto Lilienthal, the now-famous gliding expert, to learn about his theories on glider design. The industrious Pilcher returned to England and built two more gliders, including his best model, the "Hawk," before the year was out. Unlike Lilienthal, who built a hill to launch his gliders, Pilcher developed a method of towing his machines aloft. Pilcher gave considerable thought to ways to propel his gliders, and he received an English patent for a powered version of his Hawk glider. In 1899, Pilcher was working on a triplane powered by two propellers and a 4-horsepower engine. Several days before testing it, Pilcher was killed in an accident while flying his previously reliable Hawk glider. His triplane was never flown.

Short Biographies of First Flight Witnesses

An unexpected and valuable resource for the Wright brothers during their flight tests in the Outer Banks of North Carolina was the interest and assistance of the surfmen at the Kitty Hawk and Kill Devil Hills Lifesaving Stations. The brothers not only appreciated their help, they enjoyed their hospitality. Wilbur and Orville Wright earned the reputation of being polite and agreeable men who cultivated good relations with their Outer Banks neighbors. When the Wright brothers were in need of assistance, they would tack a red flag to the top of their building. It was a signal, easily seen from the Kill Devil Hills Lifesaving Station, that the brothers were going to do some flying and could use some help. Off-duty crew members, upon seeing the flag, would make the short walk over to the camp. On December 17, three surfmen would be among the five witnesses (not counting the brothers) to see history made.

Brinkley, William Cephas (1871–1940) It wasn't an interest in aviation that brought W. C. Brinkley to the Outer Banks on December 16, 1903. Brinkley, a thirty-year-old lumber buyer and part-time farmer, had come over from Manteo on Roanoke Island to search the beaches for timber washed ashore from a shipwreck a few weeks earlier. While there, he stopped by the Kill Devil Hills Lifesaving Station for conversation and a chance to warm himself. Learning that the two brothers from Dayton were going to make an attempt to fly the next day, Ceef, as he was known to friends, decided to stay the night. His curiosity was rewarded the following day when he witnessed Orville Wright's historic twelve-second flight.

Daniels, John T. (1884–1948) John Daniels, a day laborer before becoming a lifesaver in 1902, had assisted the brothers on numerous occasions. When he saw the signal flag raised on the morning of December 17, he joined a small group that headed over to the Wright brothers' camp. After assisting the Wrights in setting their 700-pound flying machine on its launch rail, Daniels was led to a camera nearby mounted on a wooden tripod. Orville charged Daniels with taking a photograph at the moment the flyer lifted off its track. Daniels, who had never taken a photograph before, carried out his duties magnificently. His "first flight" photograph would become the most famous aviation photograph ever taken. Daniels almost made history himself. After the fourth and final flight of the day, a huge gust of wind started to turn the flyer over. Grabbing one of its spars, Daniels tried to wrestle it to the ground. Instead, he found himself trapped inside the framework as it tumbled about. Having survived this scary moment, Daniels later boasted that he was the pilot on history's fifth flight. He was nearly aviation's first fatality.

Dough, William S. (1870–1931) Before becoming a surfman at the Kill Devil Hills Lifesaving Station, Dough had made his living, as so many in the area did, fishing and farming. Dough had been present on December 14, 1903, when Wilbur made his unsuccessful attempt to fly. On December 17, he joined fellow surfmen Adam Ethridge and John Daniels, who were making the short walk over to the Wright brothers' campsite in response to their signal for assistance. The thirty-four-year-old surfman helped the brothers maneuver their machine into position for an attempt to fly. Dough joined the four other men present that day as the only witnesses of the first flight.

Ethridge, Adam (1877–1940) Adam Ethridge, a surfman at the Kill Devil Hills Lifesaving Station and close friend of John Daniels, knew that something special was about to happen at Big Kill Devil Hill. In his diary entry for Sunday, December 13, Orville Wright noted that Ethridge had brought his wife and children by the campsite to see the brothers' flying machine. Several days later, Ethridge joined the small group headed to the Wright brothers' camp. Ethridge assisted in making the final preparations, then watched in wonder as Orville made history. Interestingly, Ethridge's wife was the daughter of George Westcott, victim of an Outer Banks shipwreck and grateful beneficiary of the lifesaving service.

Moore, John Thomas (1886–1952) Johnny Moore, a young man of seventeen who made his living as a trapper and crabber, had come over to Kill Devil Hills to do some fishing on December 17, 1903. The only one of the "first flight" witnesses who did not come from Manteo, Moore lived in a shack in nearby Nags Head woods. He lived there with his widowed mother, who made a living selling "quarter fortunes" to summer vacationers. Moore had stopped by the Kill Devil Hills Lifesaving Station that morning and heard the Wrights were going to attempt to fly. As he later recounted, he decided to "stick around and see the show." It was Moore who announced excitedly to those who had remained at the lifesaving station, "They done it! They done it! Damn'd if they ain't flew!" Moore would be instrumental years later in helping the government pinpoint the exact location of the first flight so that a monument could be erected to commemorate the event.

*   *   *

Bibliography

Historical References

Bernstein, Mark. *Grand Eccentrics: Turning the Century: Dayton and the Inventing of America.* Wilmington, OH: Orange Frazer Press, 1996.

Combs, Harry. *Kill Devil Hill: Discovering the Secret of the Wright Brothers.* Boston: Houghton Mifflin Company, 1979.

Crouch, Tom D. *The Bishop's Boys: A Life of Wilbur and Orville Wright.* New York: W. W. Norton & Company, 1989.

Crouch, Tom D. *A Dream of Wings: Americans and the Airplane, 1875–1905.* Washington, D.C.: Smithsonian Institution Press, 1989.

Crowther, J. G. *Six Great Inventors.* London: Hamish Hamilton, Ltd., 1954.

Culick, Fred. *On Great White Wings: The Wright Brothers and the Race for Flight.* New York: Hyperion Press, 2001.

Deines, Ann, ed. *Wilbur and Orville Wright: A Handbook of Facts.* Ft. Washington, PA: Eastern National, 2001.

Freedman, Russell. *The Wright Brothers: How They Invented the Airplane.* New York: Holiday House, 1991.

Geibert, R. *Kitty Hawk and Beyond.* Dayton, OH: Wright State University Press, 1990.

Gibbs-Smith, C. H. *The Wright Brothers: Aviation Pioneers and Their Work 1899–1911.* London: Science Museum, 2002.

Glines, Carroll V. *The Wright Brothers: Pioneers of Power Flight.* New York: Franklin Watts, Inc., 1968.

Howard, Fred. *Wilbur and Orville: A Biography of the Wright Brothers.* New York: Alfred A. Knopf, 1987.

Jakab, Peter L. *The Published Writings of Wilbur and Orville Wright.* Washington, D.C., Smithsonian Institution Press, 1990.

Jakab, Peter L. *Visions of a Flying Machine.* Washington, D.C.: Smithsonian Institution Press, 1990.

Kelly, Fred C. *How We Invented the Airplane: An Illustrated History.* New York: Dover Publications, Inc., 1989.

Kelly, Fred C., ed. *Miracle at Kitty Hawk: The Letters of Wilbur and Orville Wright.* New York: Farrar, Straus and Young, 1951.

Kelly, Fred C. *The Wright Brothers: A Biography Authorized by Orville Wright.* New York: Harcourt, Brace and Company, 1943.

McFarland, Marvin W., ed. *The Papers of Wilbur and Orville Wright.* Salem, NH: Ayer Company, 1990.

McFarland, Marvin W., ed. *The Papers of Wilbur and Orville Wright: Including the Chanute-Wright Letters and Other Papers of Octave Chanute.* New York: McGraw-Hill, 1953.

Miller, Ivonette Wright. *Wright Reminiscences.* Wright-Patterson AFB, OH: Air Force Museum Foundation, 1978.

Parramore, Tom C. *Triumph at Kitty Hawk: The Wright Brothers and Powered Flight.* Raleigh, NC: North Carolina Department of Cultural Resources, 1993.

Renstrom, Arthur. *Wilbur and Orville Wright: A Bibliography.* Washington, D.C.: Library of Congress, 1968.

Wald, Quentin. *The Wright Brothers as Engineers: An Appraisal.* Port Townsend, WA: Private printing, 1999.

Wescott, L., and Paula Degen. *Wind and Sand: The Story of the Wright Brothers at Kitty Hawk.* Ft. Washington, PA: Eastern National, 1999.

Wright, Milton. *Diaries 1857–1917.* Dayton, OH: Wright State University Libraries, 1999.

Wright, Orville. *How We Invented the Airplane: An Illustrated History.* New York: Dover Publications, Inc., 1953.

Young, Rosamond, and Catharine Fitzgerald. *Twelve Seconds to the Moon: A Story of the Wright Brothers.* Cincinnati: C. J. Krehbiel Company, 1983.

Business References

Albrecht, Karl. *Brain Power: Learn to Improve Your Thinking Skills.* New York: Simon & Schuster, 1992.

Albrecht, Karl. *The Power of Minds at Work: Organizational Intelligence in Action*. New York: AMACOM, 2002.

Deal, Terrence, and Allan A. Kennedy. *Corporate Cultures: The Rites and Rituals of Corporate Life*. New York: Perseus Publishing, 2000.

Eppler, Mark. *Management Mess-Ups: 57 Pitfalls You Can Avoid (and Stories of Those Who Didn't)*. Franklin Lakes, NJ: Career Press, 1998.

Galford, Robert, and Anne Seibold Drapeau. *The Trusted Leader: Bringing Out the Best in Your People and Your Company*. New York: Free Press, 2003.

Gootnick, Mary, and David Gootnick. *Action Tools for Effective Managers: A Guide for Solving Day-to-Day Problems on the Job*. New York: AMACOM, 2002.

Kayser, Thomas A. *Mining Group Gold: How to Cash In on the Collaborative Brain Power of a Group*. New York: McGraw-Hill Trade, 1995.

MacMillan, Pat. *The Performance Factor: Unlocking the Secrets of Teamwork*. Nashville, TN: Broadman & Holman Publishers, 2001.

Michalko, Michael. *Thinkertoys: A Handbook of Business Creativity*. Berkeley, CA: Ten Speed Press, 1991.

Mitchell, Donald, Carol Coles, and Robert Metz. *The 2,000 Percent Solution: Free Your Organization from "Stalled" Thinking to Achieve Organizational Success*. New York: AMACOM, 1999.

Peters, Tom. *The Circle of Innovation*. New York: Alfred A. Knopf, 1997.

Ryan, Kathleen, and Daniel K. Oestreich. *Driving Fear Out of the Workplace: Creating the High-Trust, High-Performance Organization*. San Francisco, CA: Jossey-Bass Publishers, 1998.

Tobin, Daniel R. *The Knowledge-Enabled Organization: Moving from "Training" to "Learning" to Meet Business Goals*. New York: AMACOM, 1998.

Von Oech, Roger. *A Whack on the Side of the Head: How to Unlock Your Mind for Innovation*. New York: Warner Books, 1998.

*　　*　　*

Glossary of Aviation Terms

Ailerons　The movable part of an airplane wing used to generate a rolling motion, a necessary factor in establishing lateral control. This rolling motion was achieved by the Wright brothers through the use of their wing-warping system.

Airfoil　A body, such as a wing or propeller blade, designed to provide a desired reaction force when in motion relative to the surrounding air. The amount of lift or thrust generated depends on the shape of the airfoil.

Angle of incidence   Also known as the angle of attack, this is the angle created between the chord (width) of the wing and the direction of relative wind. Changing the angle of incidence changes the amount of lift generated by a wing (the greater the angle, the greater the lift). A stall can occur if the angle is too great.

Anhedral   The angle created when two surfaces meet and the angle of the lower sides is less than 180 degrees. This is best recognized by the downward (drooping) slope of the wings. The Wright brothers' 1903 *Flyer* featured anhedral wings in an effort to induce roll.

Chord   The straight line joining the leading and trailing lines of an airfoil (wing).

Control   The ability to maintain the attitude (orientation) of an aircraft in all three dimensions (axes) of flight: roll, pitch, and yaw. This was the major breakthrough of the Wright brothers and the basis of their patent.

Dihedral   The angle created when two surfaces meet and the angle of the upper sides is less than 180 degrees. This is best recognized as the upward slope of an aircraft's wings. A dihedral angle adds roll stability to the wings.

Drag   The resistance created as an object moves through the air. The amount of thrust generated by the propulsion system must be greater than the amount of drag to achieve and sustain flight. The goal is to minimize drag as much as possible, which is why the Wright brothers initially flew in a prone position.

Elevator   A movable surface used to control pitch. On the 1903 *Wright Flyer,* the elevator (called a canard) was placed in front of the aircraft to protect the pilot. Today, it is located in the rear of an airplane, attached to the horizontal stabilizer.

Lateral equilibrium   Also called lateral control, this is the state an aircraft achieves when its wings are held steady. It is the absence of roll.

Lift   To make an airplane fly, sufficient force (i.e., lift) must be generated to overcome the plane's weight. This is the basis of flight. Air passing over the top surface of a wing travels a greater distance than the air going under it due to the curvature (camber) of the wing. This creates a difference in pressure that allows the wing to generate lift.

Ornithopter   Term applied to all flying machines propelled or supported by the flapping motion of wings. Otto Lilienthal was the last major proponent of this method of powering a craft.

Pitch   The movement of an airplane's nose up or down. Pitch was controlled initially by the Wright brothers through the use of a forward elevator. Today it is accomplished by a horizontal stabilizer in the rear of the aircraft.

Propeller   A shaft made of long, twisted pieces of metal or wood that are turned at a high rate of speed. The motion of propellers creates the thrust needed to overcome resistance or drag.

Roll   The up-and-down movement of the wing tips. Roll can best be envisioned as the movement of the wings when a pilot wants to "wave" from the sky. The Wright brothers achieved roll by wing-warping.

Rudder   The movable surfaces located at the rear of the aircraft and controlled by the pilot. The rudder is used to control yaw (side-to-side movement). Today, it's part of the aircraft's vertical stabilizer.

Stability   An aircraft that tends to return to steady flight after a disturbance is said to be stable. The Wright brothers dealt with this problem (inherent instability) by giving the pilot a means to control the aircraft in all three axes.

Stall   This occurs when the angle of incidence becomes too great and air cannot move freely under the wing. The Wright brothers referred to this as "well-digging." It is also known as tailspin.

Thrust   The mechanical force needed to overcome drag. Most airplanes have some kind of propulsion system to generate this force. Thrust was achieved by the Wright brothers with two pusher-style propellers powered by a 12-horsepower engine.

Wing   One of the airfoils that develops the lift needed to achieve and sustain flight. The shape of the wing (i.e., its camber) is one of the major factors affecting lift and drag. The distance between the leading and trailing edge of the wing is its chord; the distance from wing tip to wing tip is its span.

Wing-warping   A system developed by the Wright brothers to control the roll of the aircraft by changing (twisting) the shape of the wing tips while in flight. Today, aircraft achieve this effect by moving sections of the wing called ailerons and spoilers.

Yaw   The movement of an airplane's nose from side to side. If you picture an axle running through the top of the plane, this is the movement that would be created by rotating on that axle.

Note: The Glenn Research Center at NASA has an excellent website that uses Java simulation to show the actual effect of control features (e.g., ailerons, wing-warping, rudder, elevator, etc.). For those interested in learning more about how these elements interact, visit its website at www.lerc.nasa.gov/WWW/K-12/airplane/bga.html.

INDEX

visionaries, 86
Visions of a Flying Machine, x, 28, 139,
    141, 153, 179

weight, 65, 66
Western Society of Engineers, 62
what–if questions, 88
whole–world vision, 110
Whitehead, Alfred North, 50
Wilbur and Orville, 44, 83, 169–170
wind tunnel
    description of, 145
    experiments, 144–146
wing design, 54, 69, 80
wing warping, *see* torsioning
Wright, Bishop 151
Wright Brothers, The, 23, 96, 191–192
Wright brothers
    achievements of, *vii–viii*
    business ventures of, 116
    childhood of, 78–81
    debates of, 41–44
    decision of who should fly first,
        154–155
    determination of, 172
    diligence in research of, 120
    early interest in flight, 2–3, 7, 78
    education, 115–117
    flying together, 184–185
    and fiddling, 82
    first cooperative project of, 82
    flexible approach of, 105
    and forging, 45–46
    impact on economy, 20
    innovations of, 67, 80–81, 141
    passion of, 175
    reasons for success of, 8–9, 17–21,
        34, 175
    skills of, 10
    teamwork of, 9, 152
    work objectives of, 137–138

Wright, Catharine, 62–63
Wright Cycle Company, 44
Wright family, 114, 118, 140
Wright Flyer, x–xi, xv, 33, 135–136, 180
Wright, John Loyd, 85
Wright, Lorin, 54
Wright, Milton, 36, 43, 78–79, 117,
    180, 182
    dairy excerpts of, 134–135
Wright, Orville
    on accomplishment, 163–164
    diary excerpts of, 131–132
    importance of appearance to, 63
    inventions of, 78, 80–81
    on lateral equilibrium, 100
    personal attributes of, 5–6
    resourcefulness of, 82
    on Smithsonian controversy, 33
    after Wilbur's death, 183
    vision of success of, 173
Wright Reminiscences, ix, 5, 6–7, 46, 59
Wright, Susan Catherine, 36
Wright, Wilbur
    addressing the Western Society of
        Engineers, 62–64
    on ambition, 114
    on balance, 61
    early interest in flying, 7
    on "dishonest" arguments, 55–56
    on fame and fortune, 67
    on genius factor, 37
    on instability of flight, 98
    inventions of, 80–81
    last will of, 166
    on lateral balance of birds, 99–100
    on Lilienthal, 119, 143
    on methodology, 133
    personal attributes of, 7
    skating accident of, 168

Young, Rosamund, 121

ABOUT MARK EPPLER

Mark Eppler is a professional speaker and seminar leader specializing in leadership, management, and communication issues. An award-winning university adjunct, Mark has taught courses in business and management at Indiana University, his alma mater. In addition, he has 20 years experience at the executive level in the electronics industry, most recently as president and chief operating officer of a component manufacturer.

Although Mark's interest in the Wright brothers dates back two decades, it wasn't until 1995 that he began incorporating their story into his seminars and workshops. Interest grew into passion as he discovered a wealth of practical advice contained in the inspiring accomplishments of the two men. The principles that emerged in Mark's programs became the inspiration for *The Wright Way*.

Mark is the author of *Management Mess-Ups: 57 Pitfalls You Can Avoid (And Stories of Those Who Didn't),* now in its fifth printing, including a Chinese language edition. A graduate of Indiana University, Mark lives in Milford, Ohio, with his wife and trusted advisor, Linda. He can be contacted at:

Mark Eppler & Associates
126 Lakefield Drive
Milford, OH 45150-1884

Phone: 513-576-9746
E-mail: mark@markeppler.com